Coloring Books

Coloring Book

I0833176

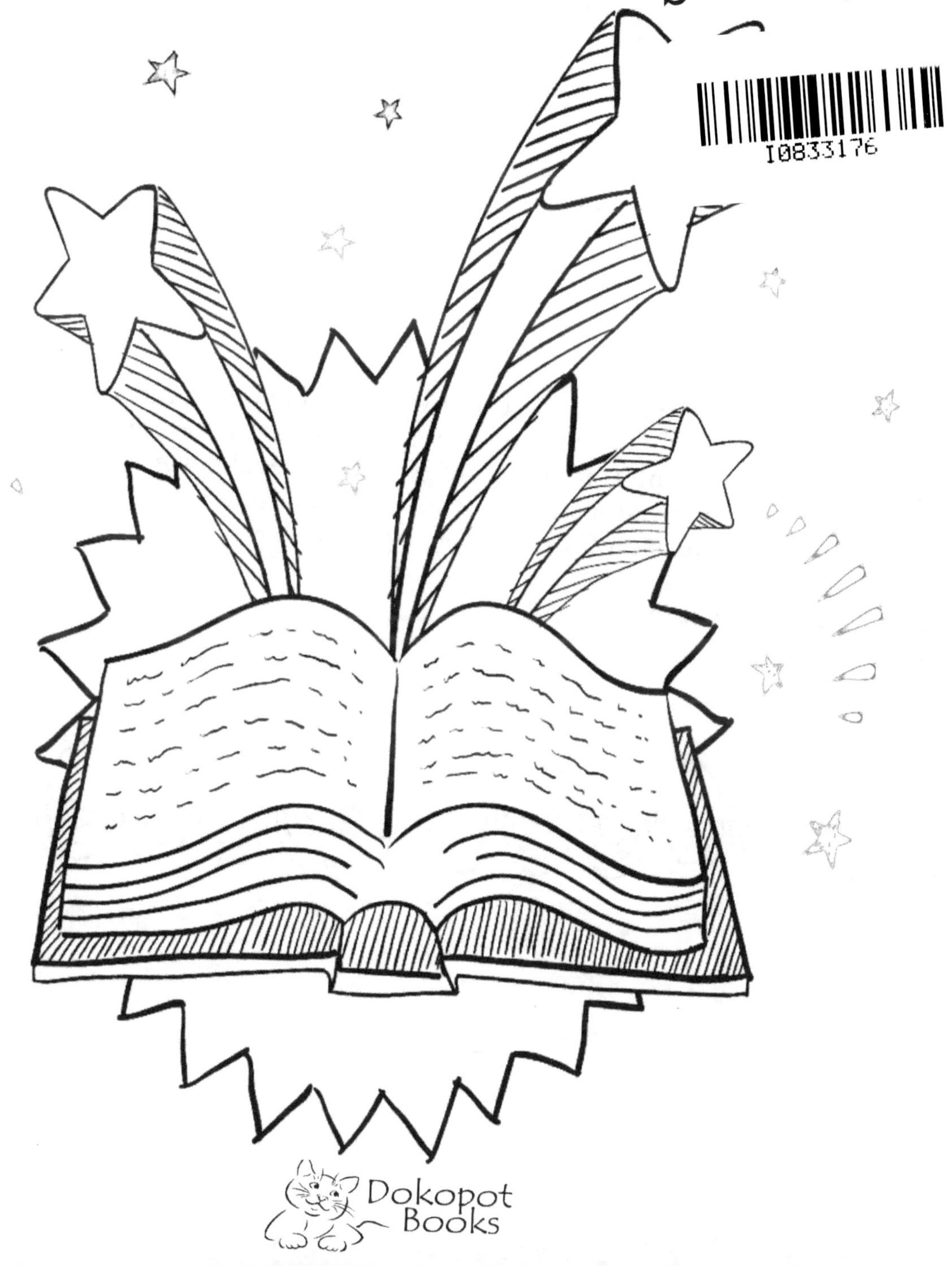

Dokopot Books

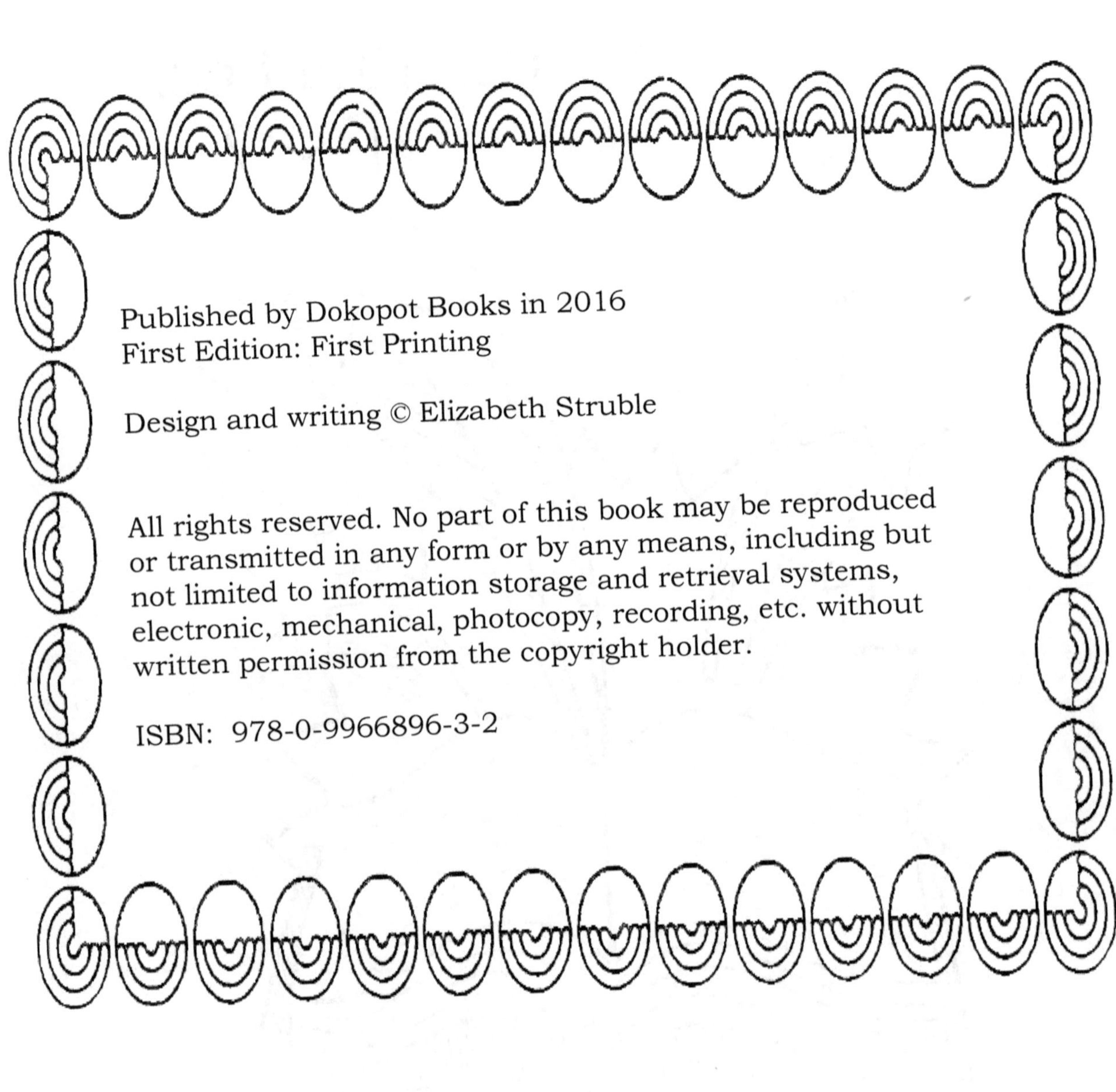

Published by Dokopot Books in 2016
First Edition: First Printing

ISBN: 978-0-9966896-3-2

Dedication

For lovers of books
and color,
explore
and enjoy!

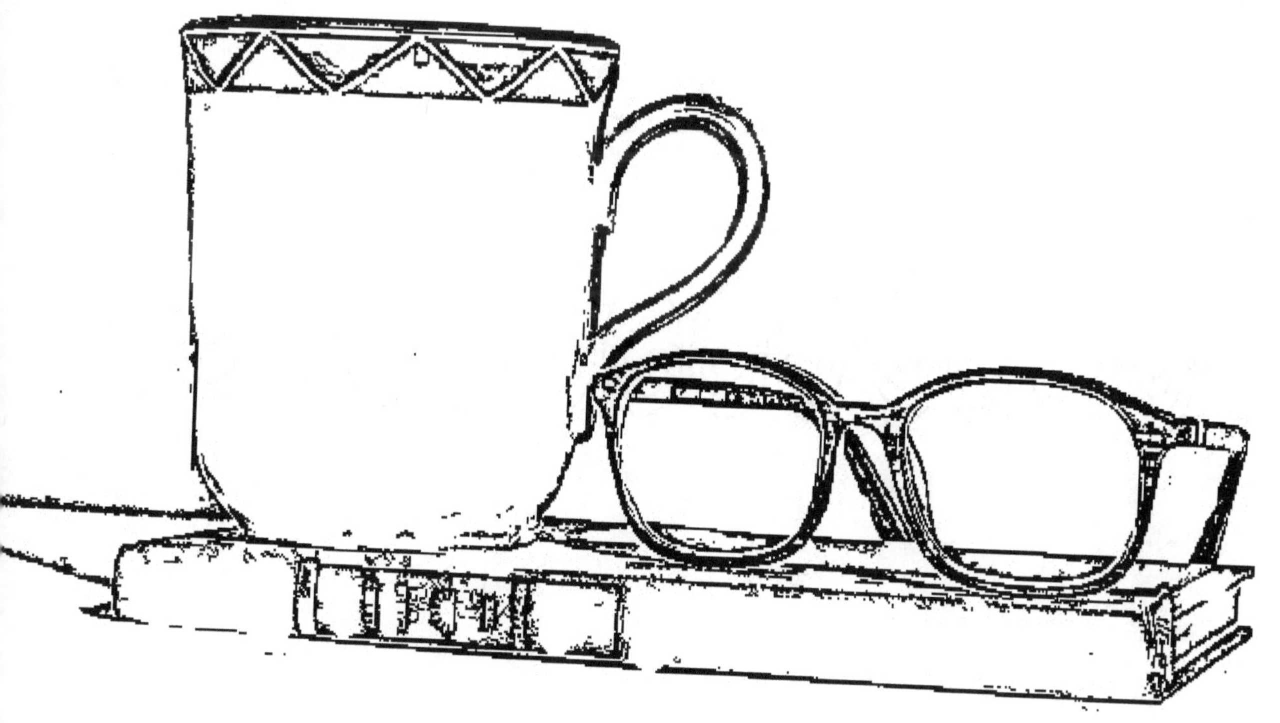

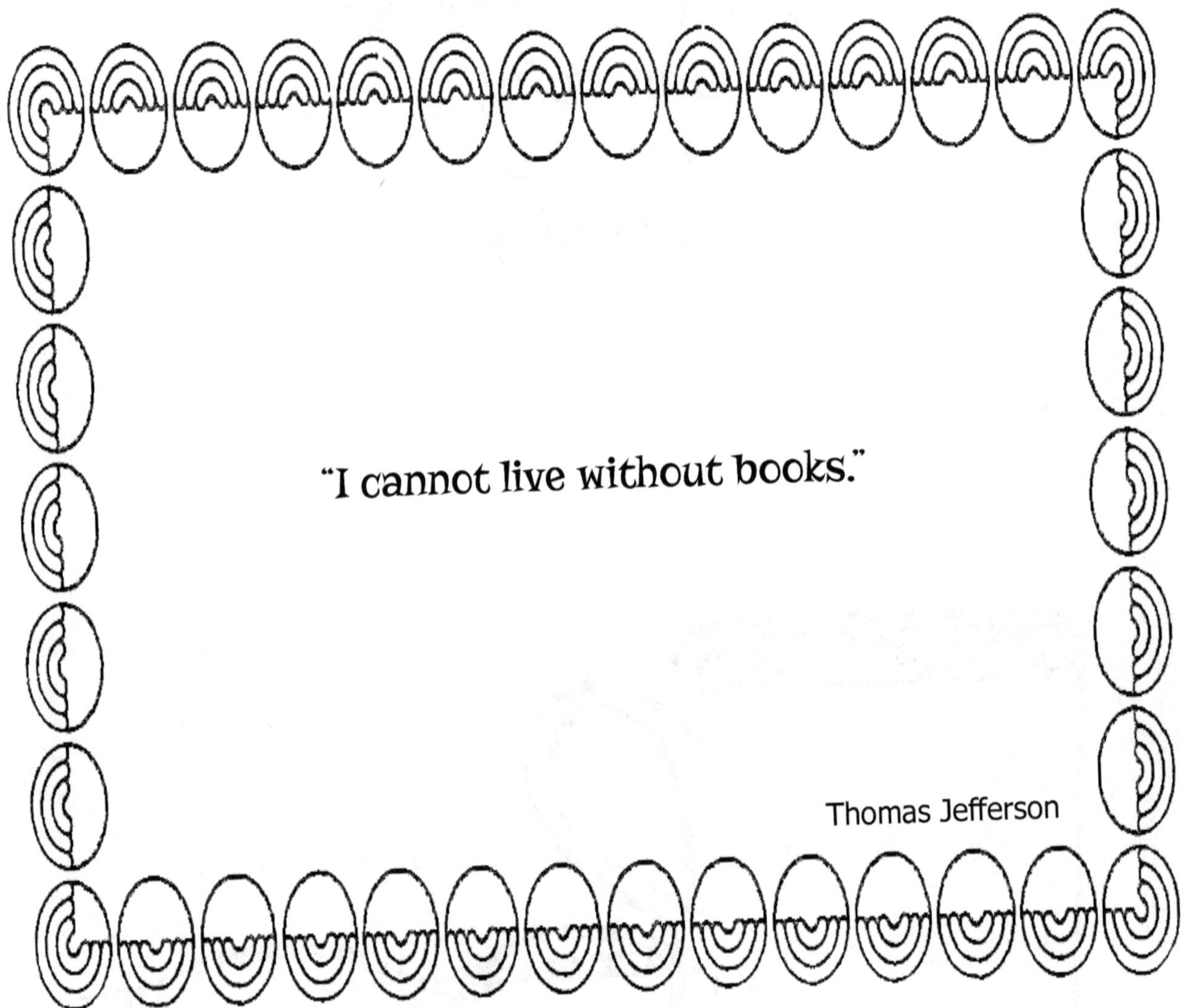
"I cannot live without books."
Thomas Jefferson

Suggestions for using this coloring book:

- The designs in this collection are created in a variety of styles. From easy pictures that might remind you of a favorite childhood coloring book to complicated, abstract designs, you're sure to find plenty to like--and to color.

- Use colored pencils, pens, markers, pastels, or even the old, forgotten colors hiding in a drawer somewhere. Any medium works for these pages. Use your favorites or, even better, try coloring with something new.

- These coloring pages are printed on one side only but do place a sheet of paper or thin card stock behind the page as you color to prevent possible bleed through.

- There are no rights or wrongs in coloring. Be as perfect or imperfect as you wish. Enjoy yourself!

- Think about the book quotes as you color. If you wish, write your own thoughts and feelings in the space around the quote.

- Coloring has been proven to lower stress and reduce anxiety. With this meditative, soothing activity you'll be freeing your mind, senses and creativity.

•

- Now, go forth and COLOR!

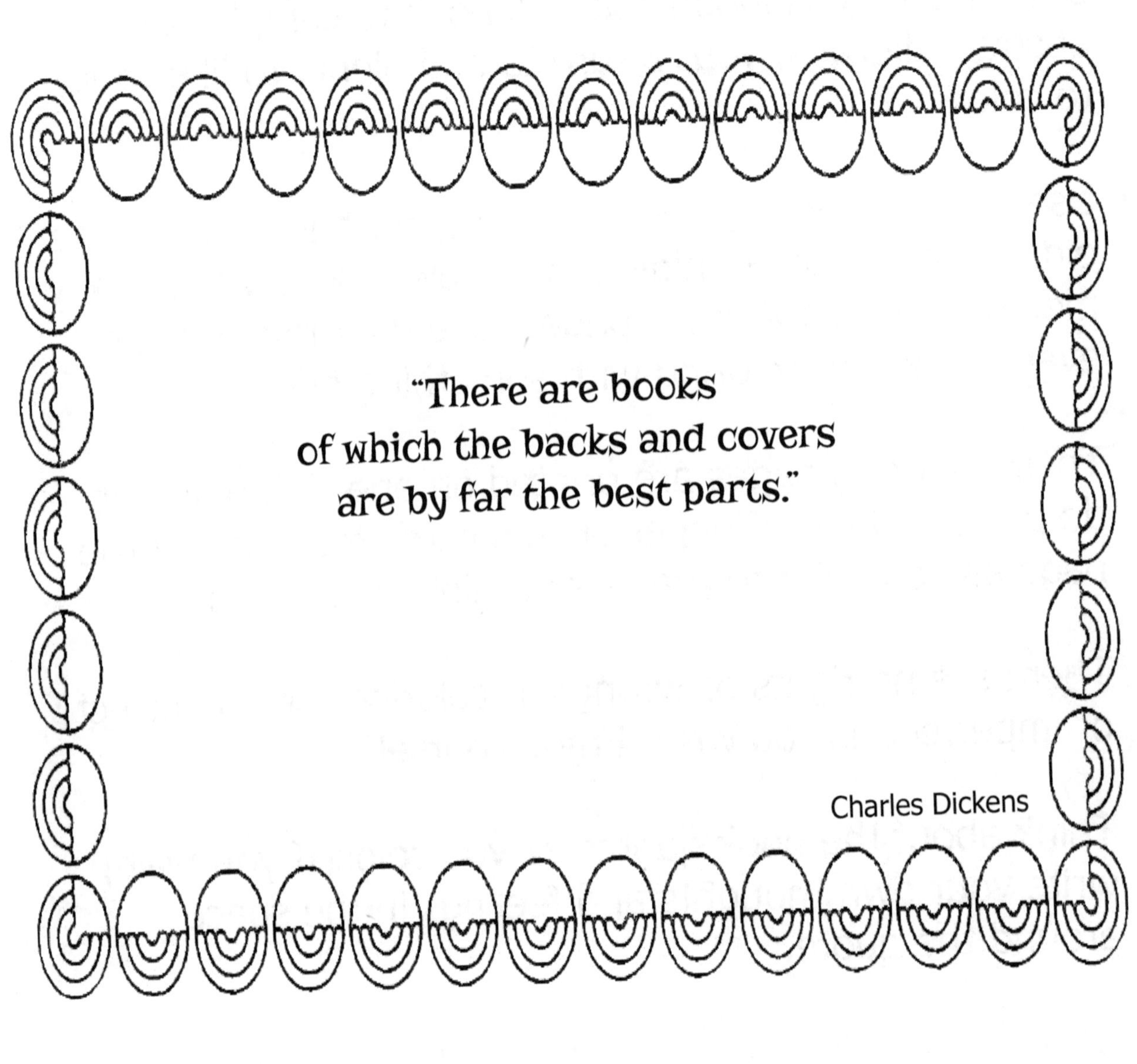

"There are books
of which the backs and covers
are by far the best parts."

Charles Dickens

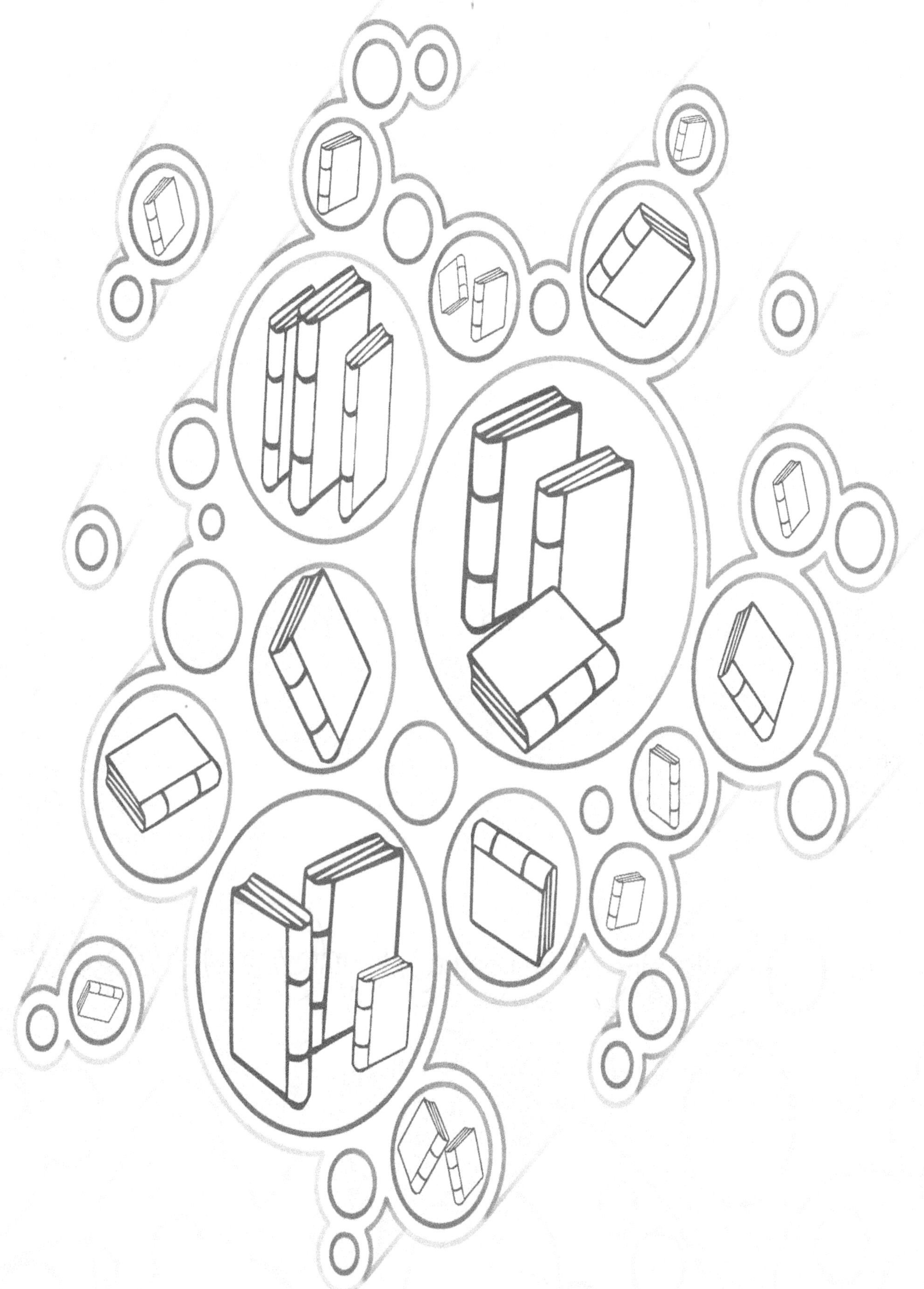

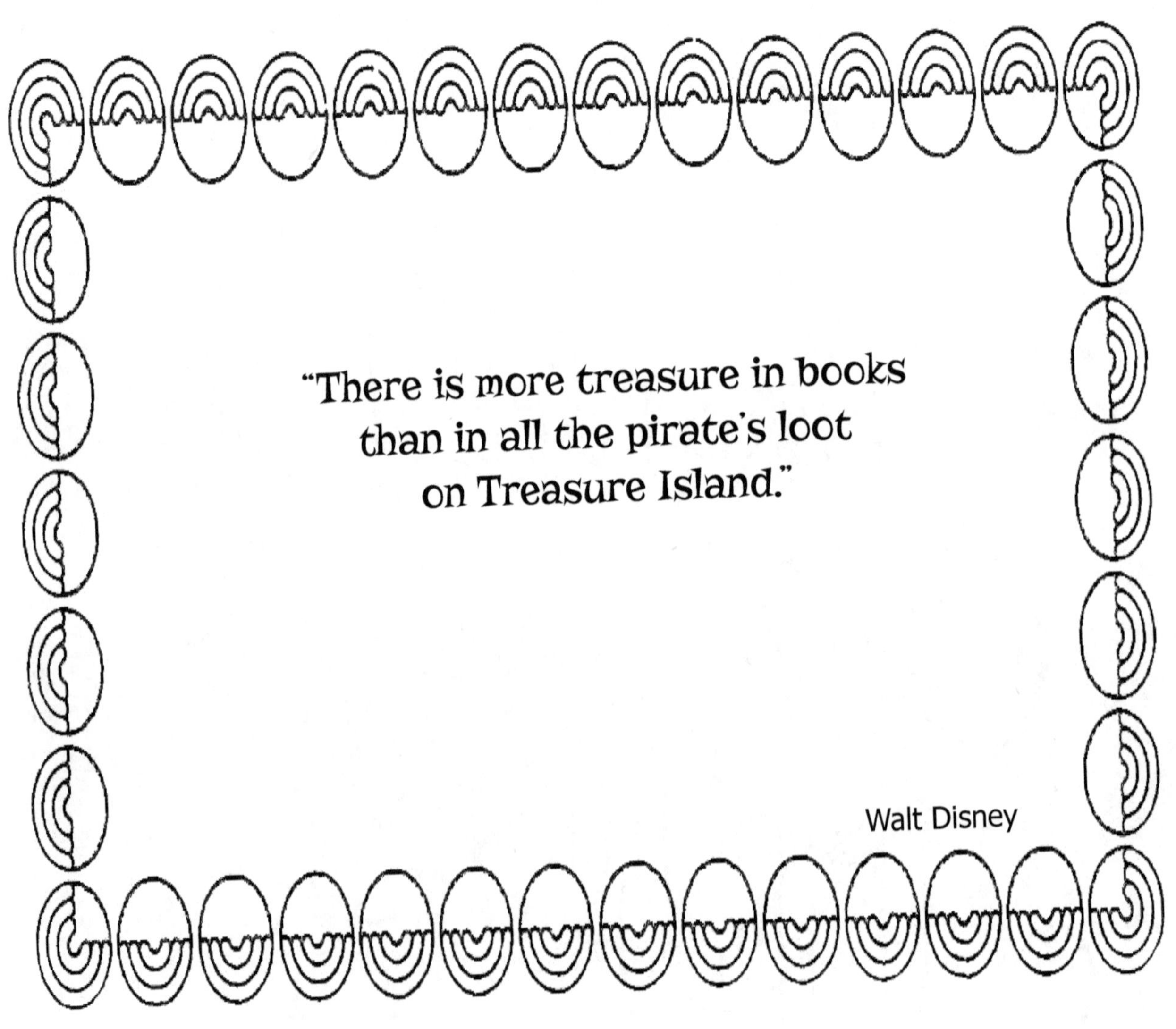
"There is more treasure in books
than in all the pirate's loot
on Treasure Island."
Walt Disney

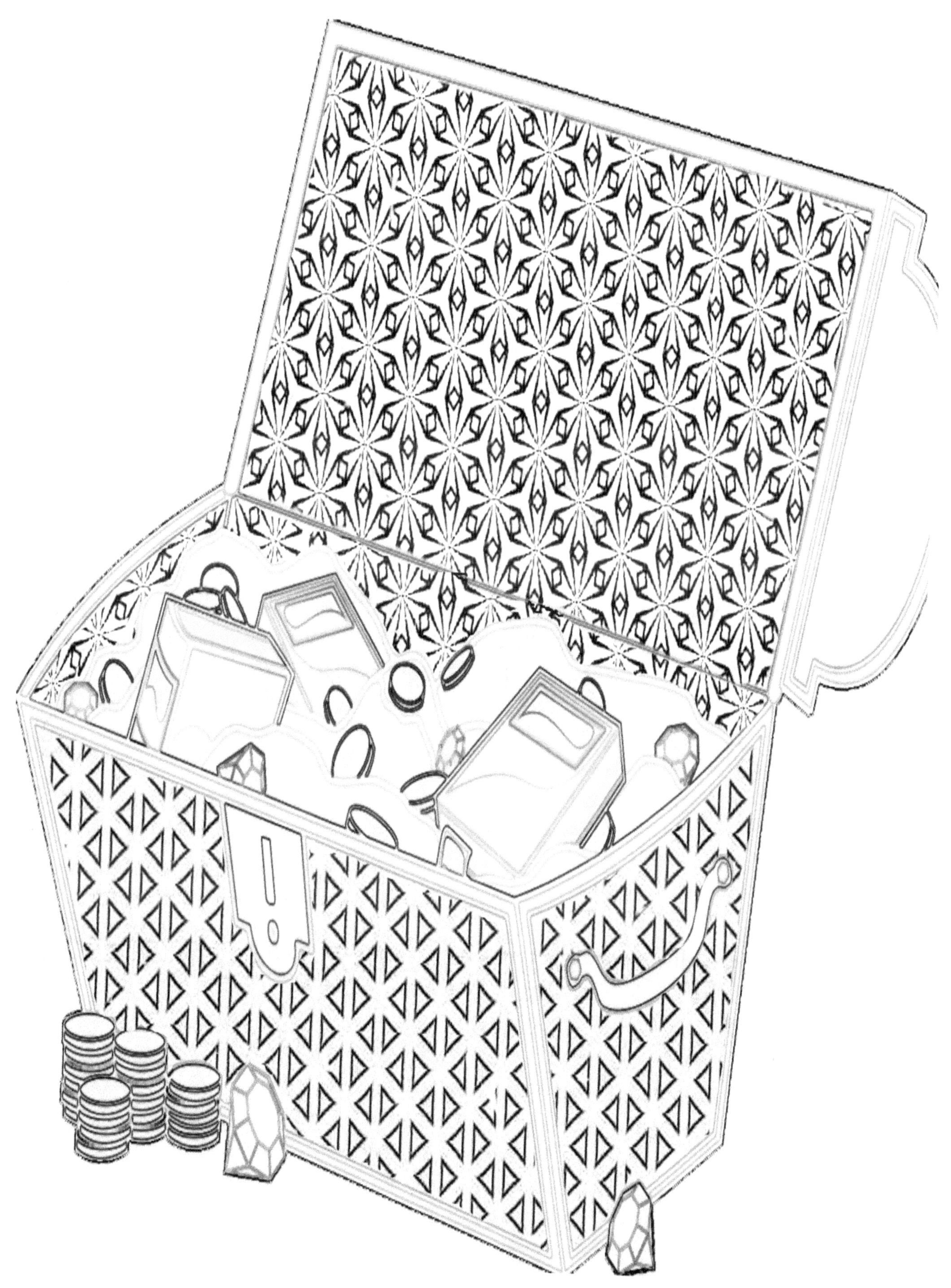

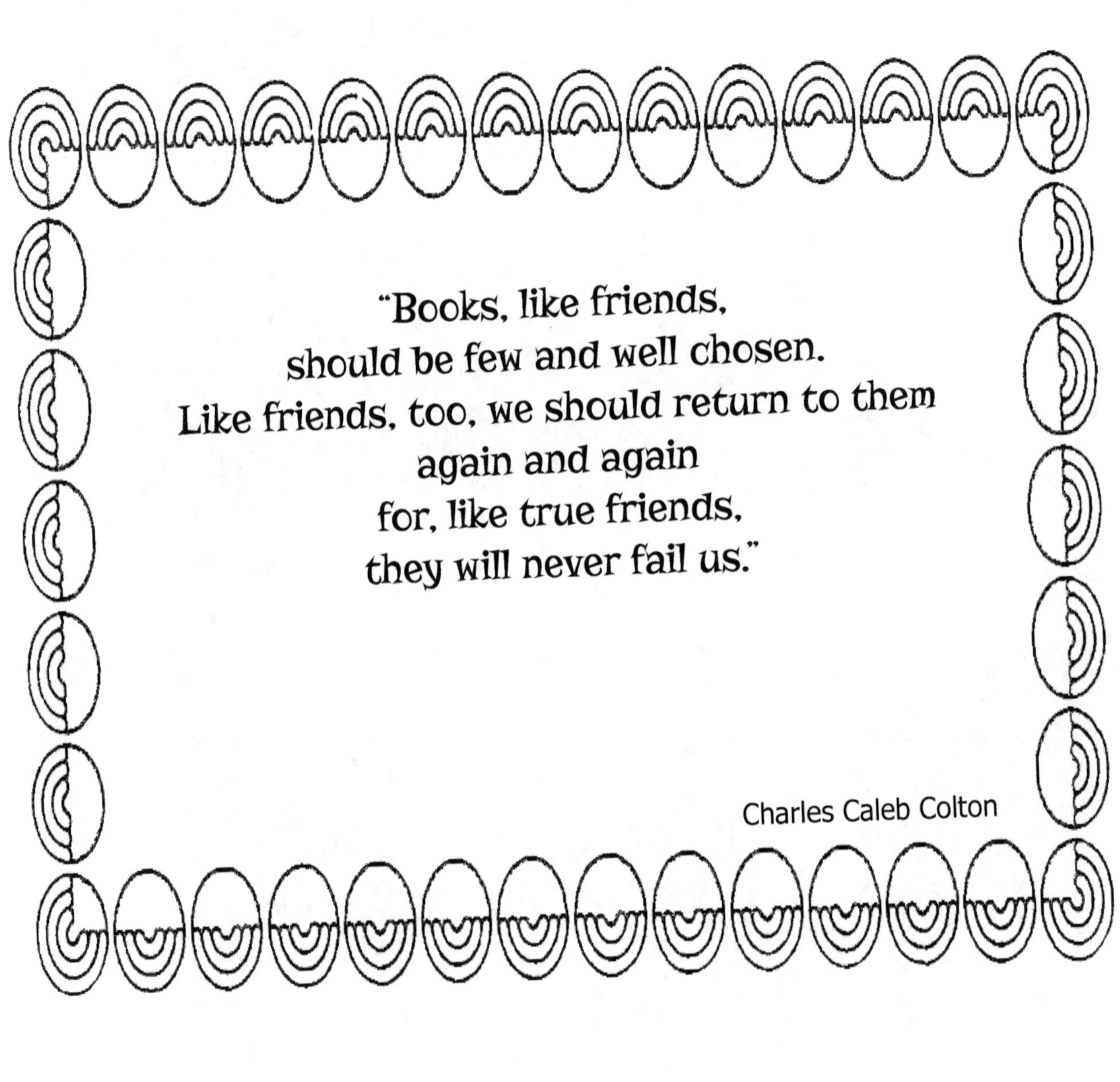
"Books, like friends,
should be few and well chosen.
Like friends, too, we should return to them
again and again
for, like true friends,
they will never fail us."
Charles Caleb Colton

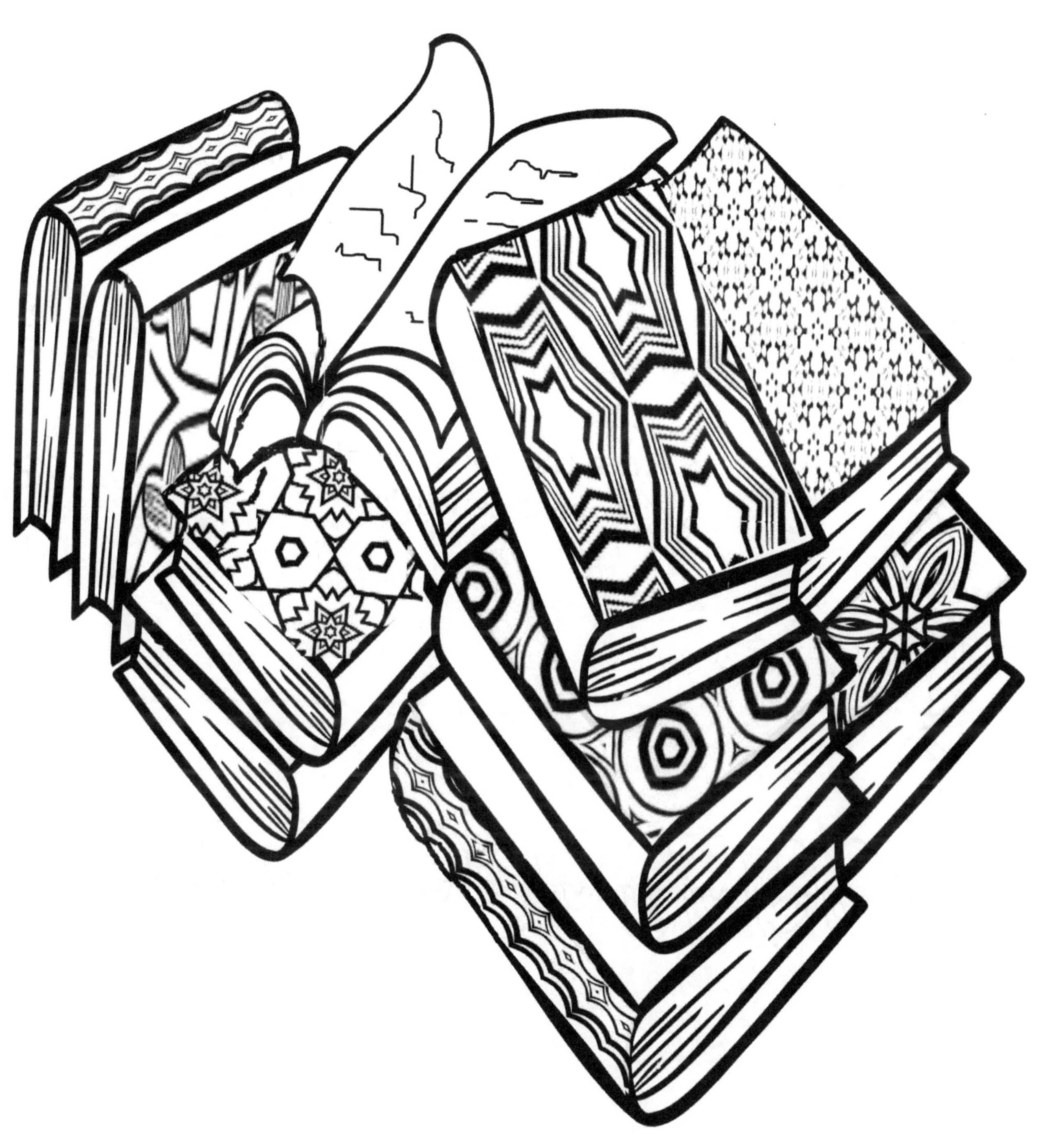

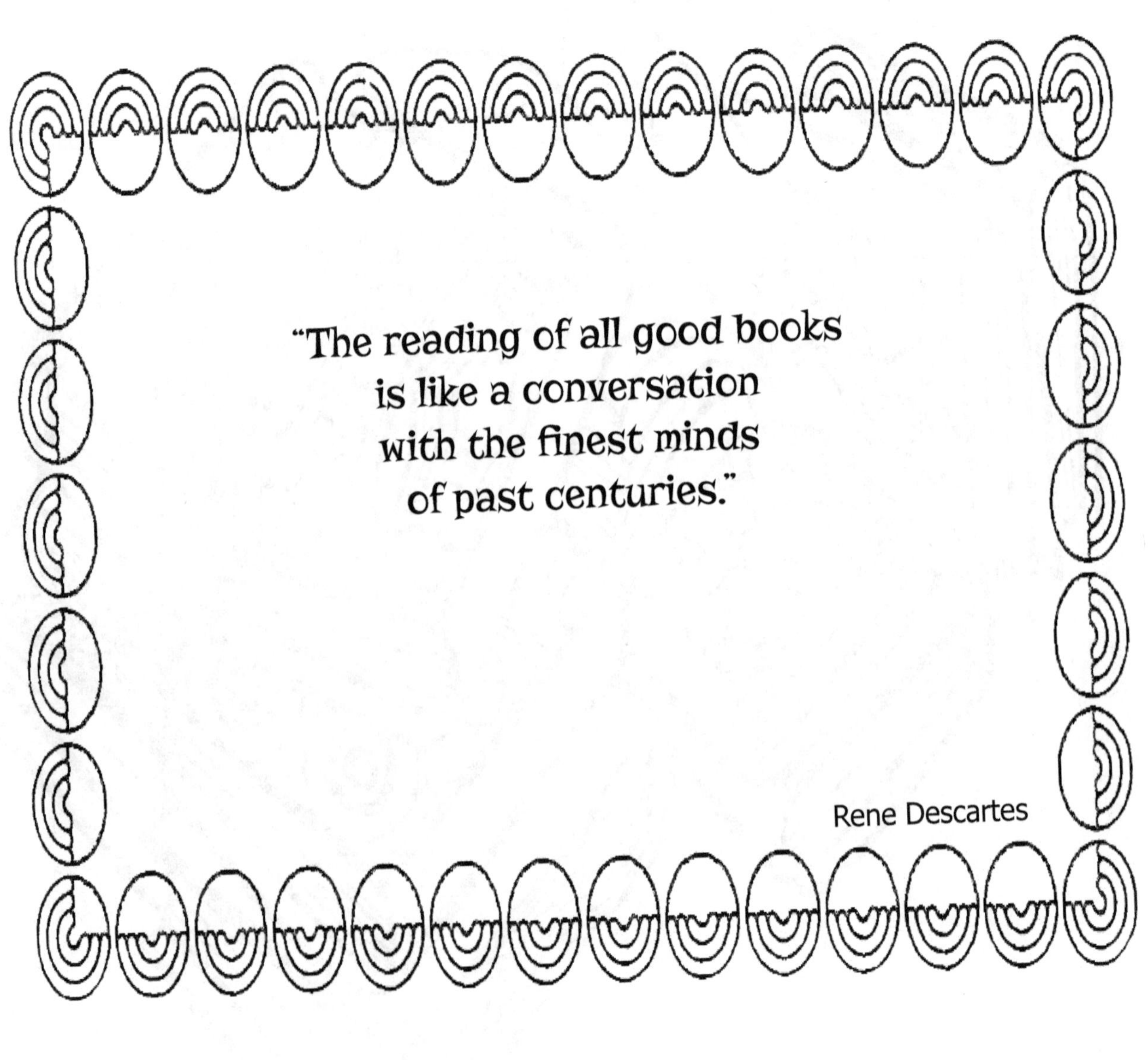

"The reading of all good books
is like a conversation
with the finest minds
of past centuries."

Rene Descartes

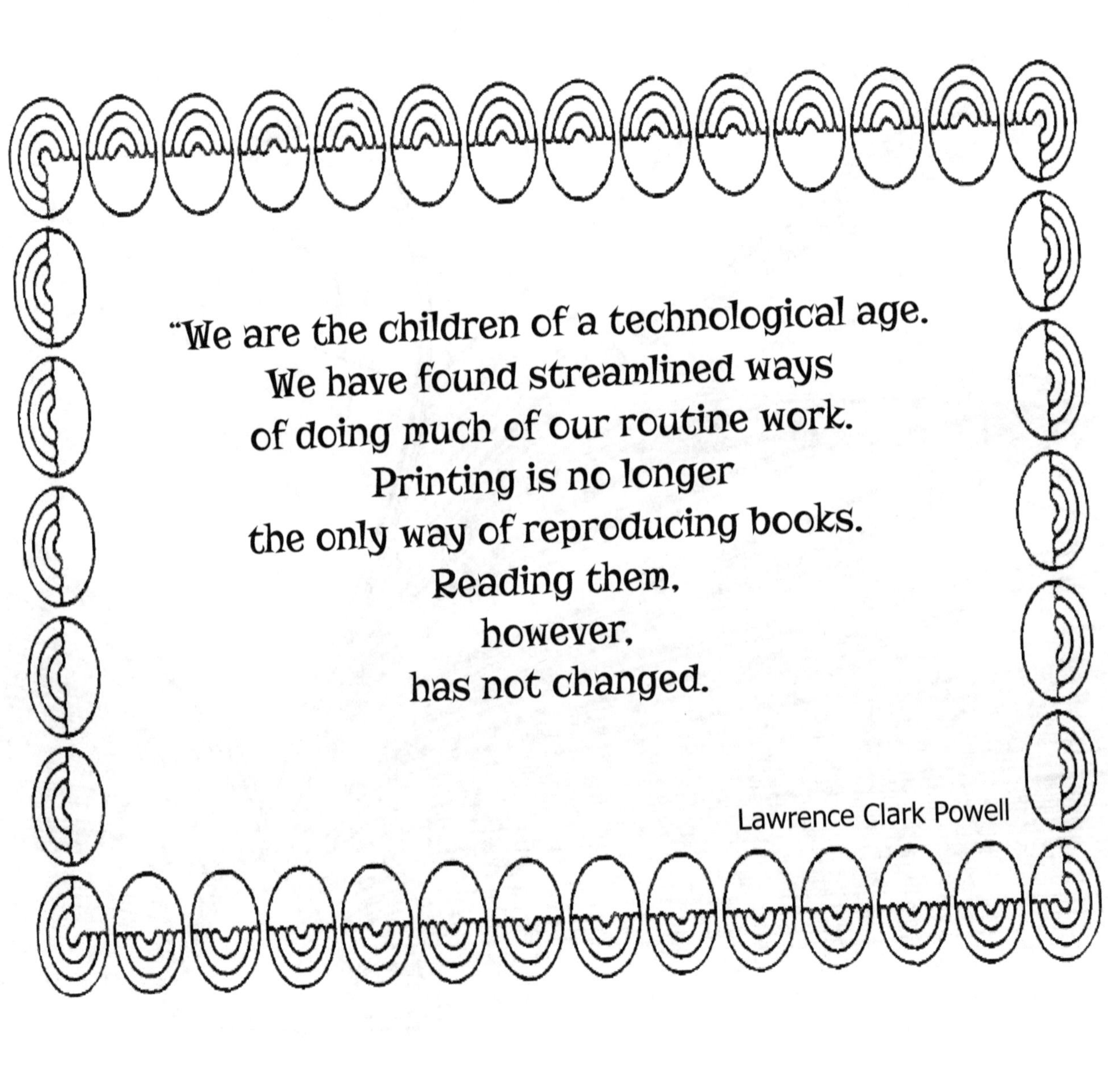

"We are the children of a technological age.
We have found streamlined ways
of doing much of our routine work.
Printing is no longer
the only way of reproducing books.
Reading them,
however,
has not changed.

Lawrence Clark Powell

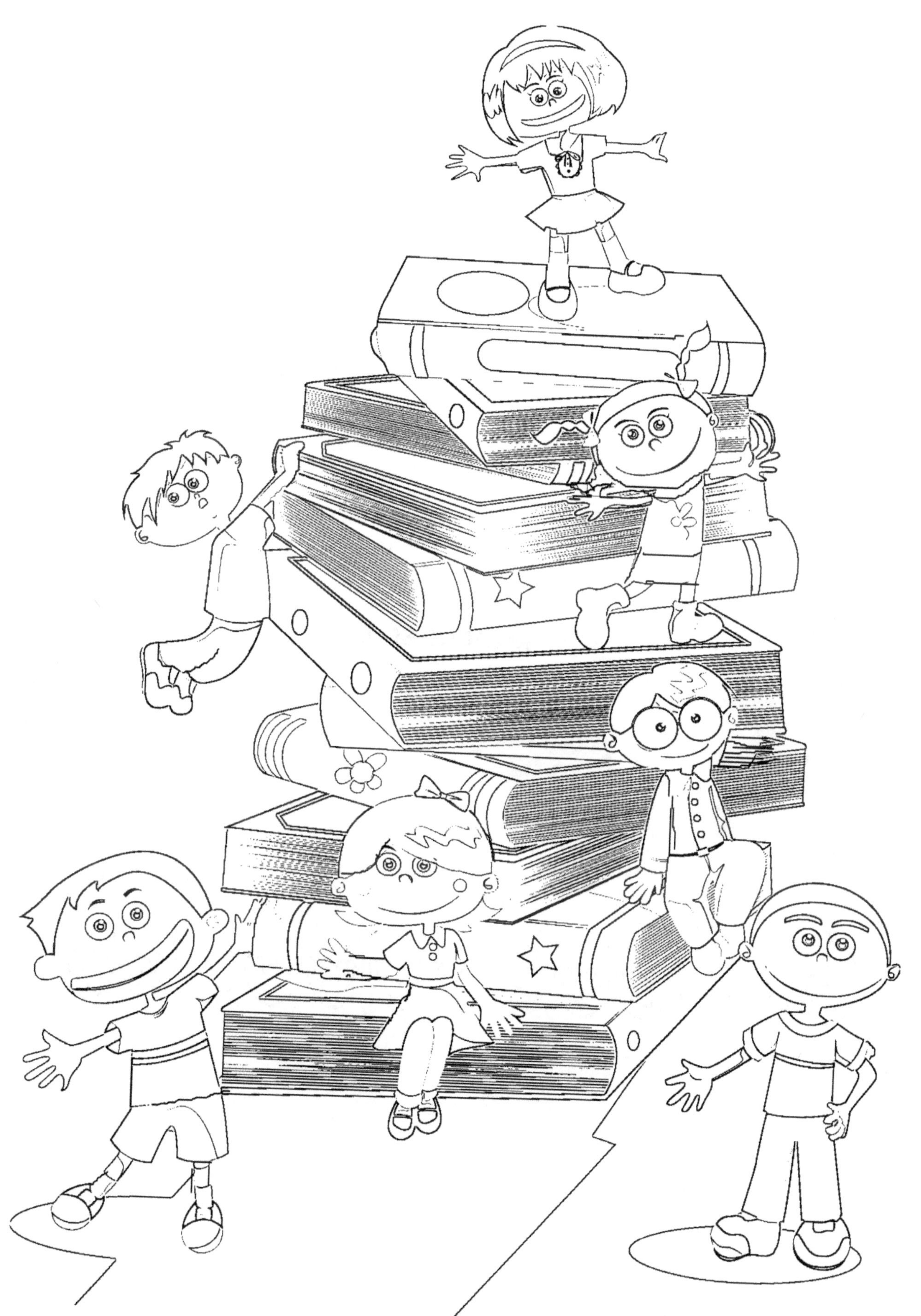

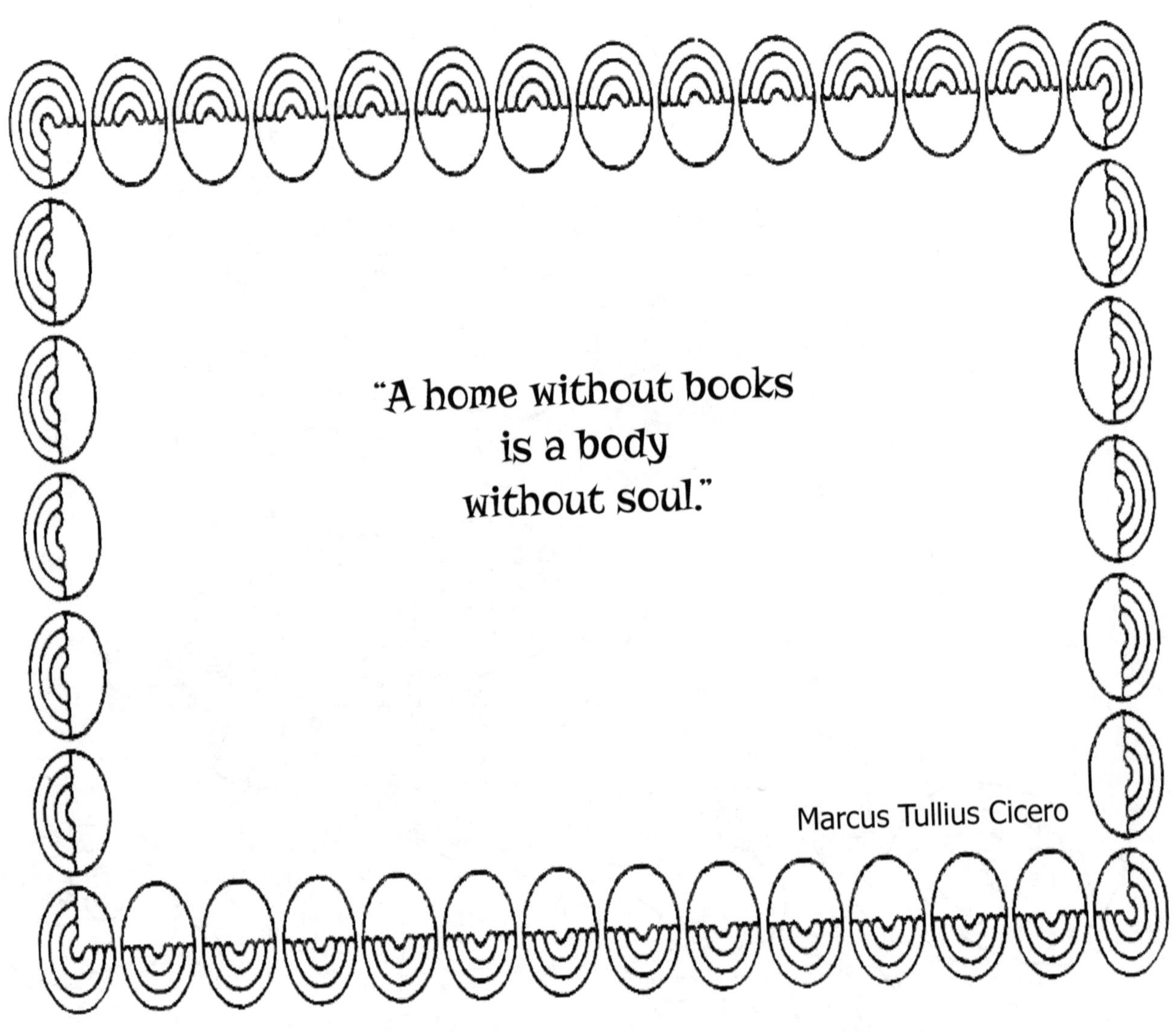

"A home without books
is a body
without soul."

Marcus Tullius Cicero

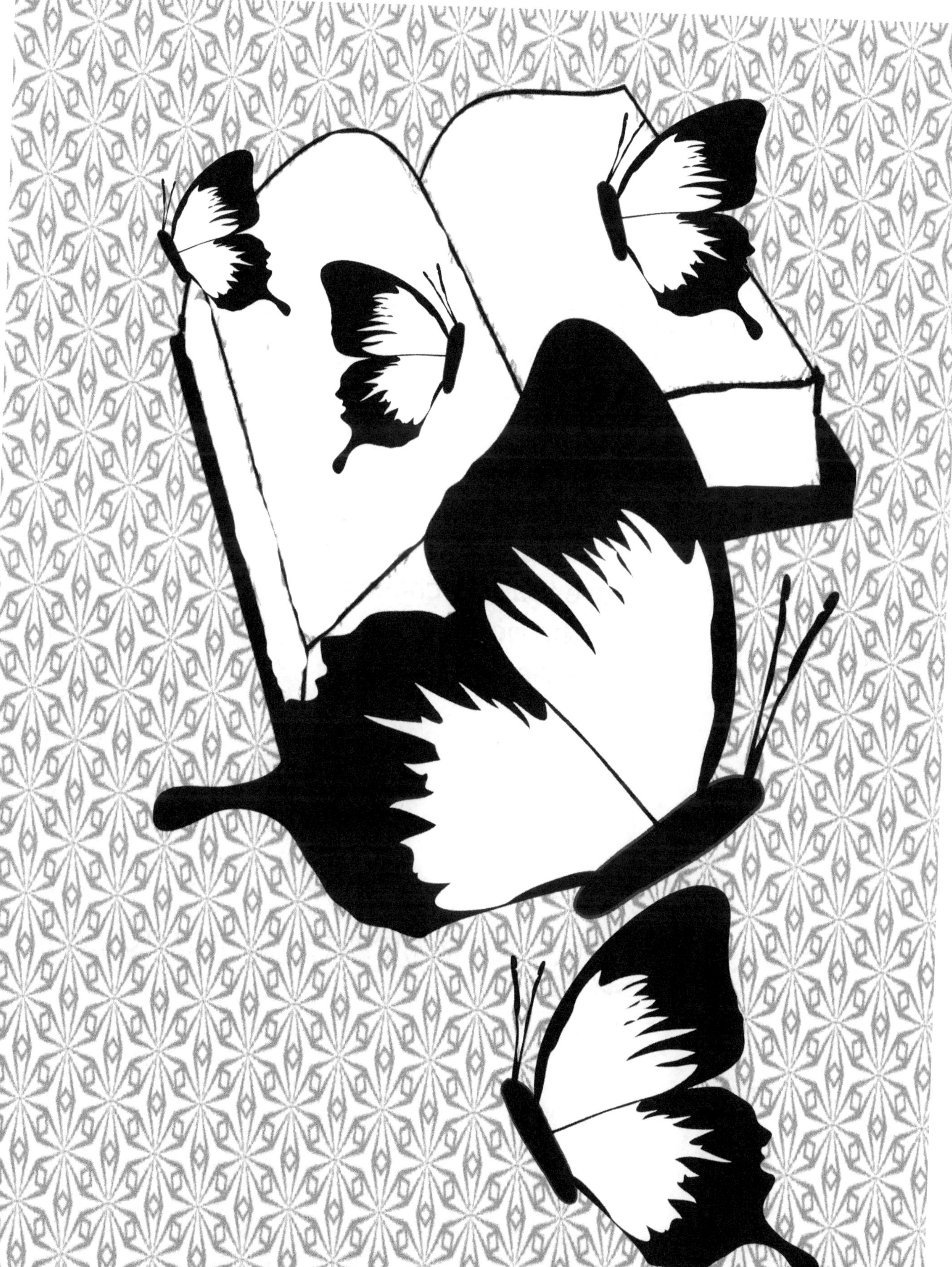

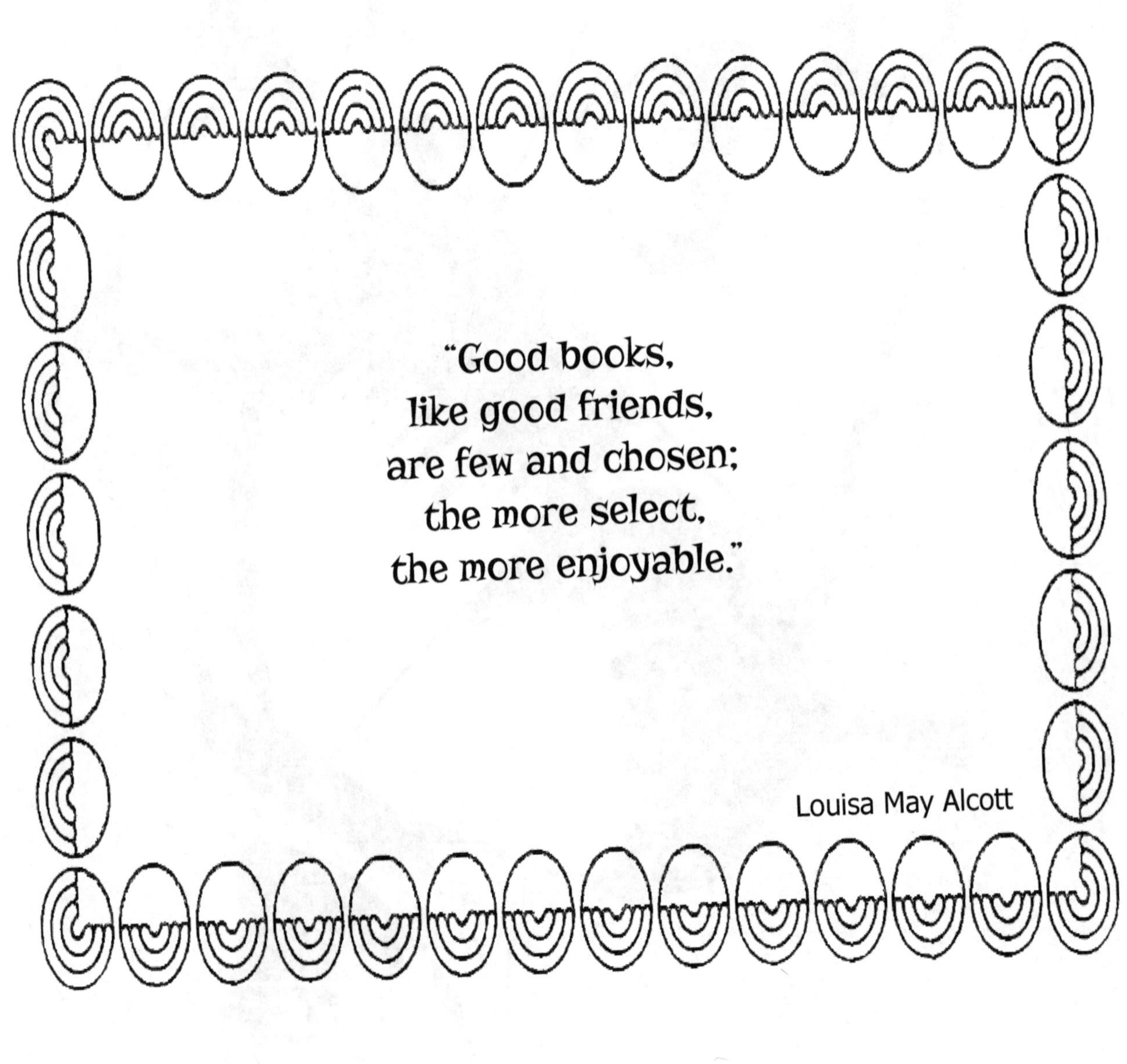
"Good books,
like good friends,
are few and chosen;
the more select,
the more enjoyable."
Louisa May Alcott

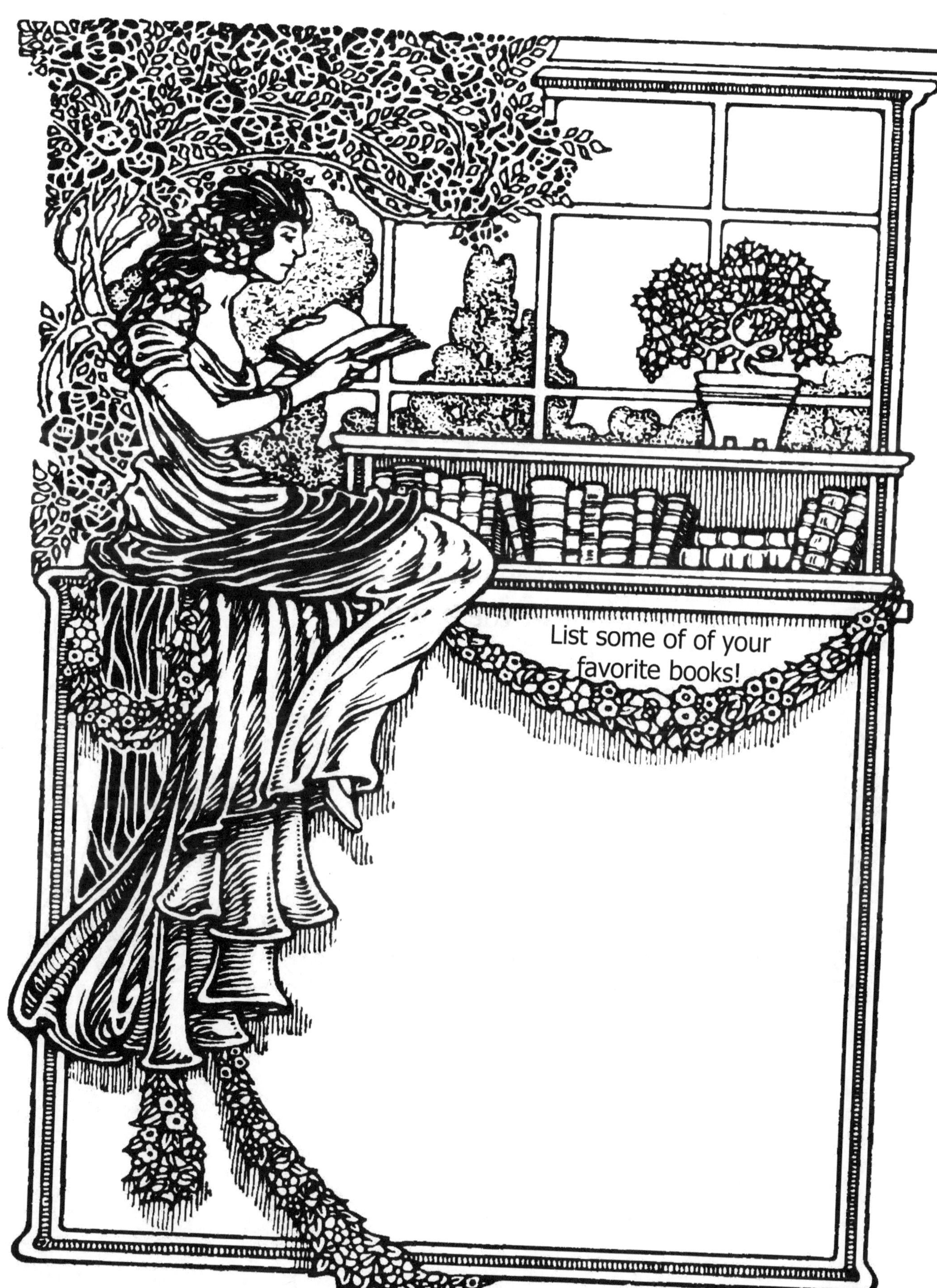
List some of of your
favorite books!

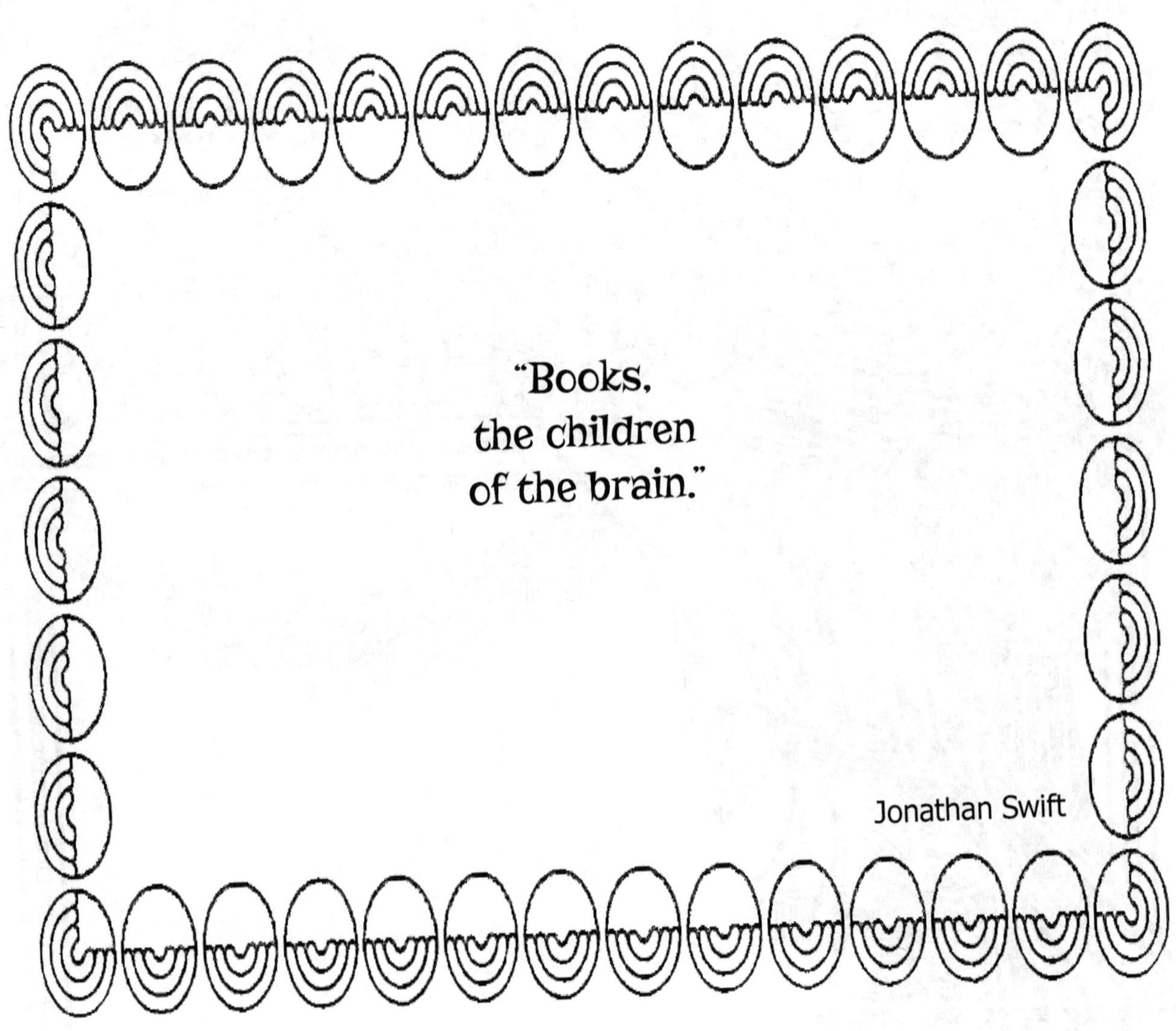

"Books,
the children
of the brain."

Jonathan Swift

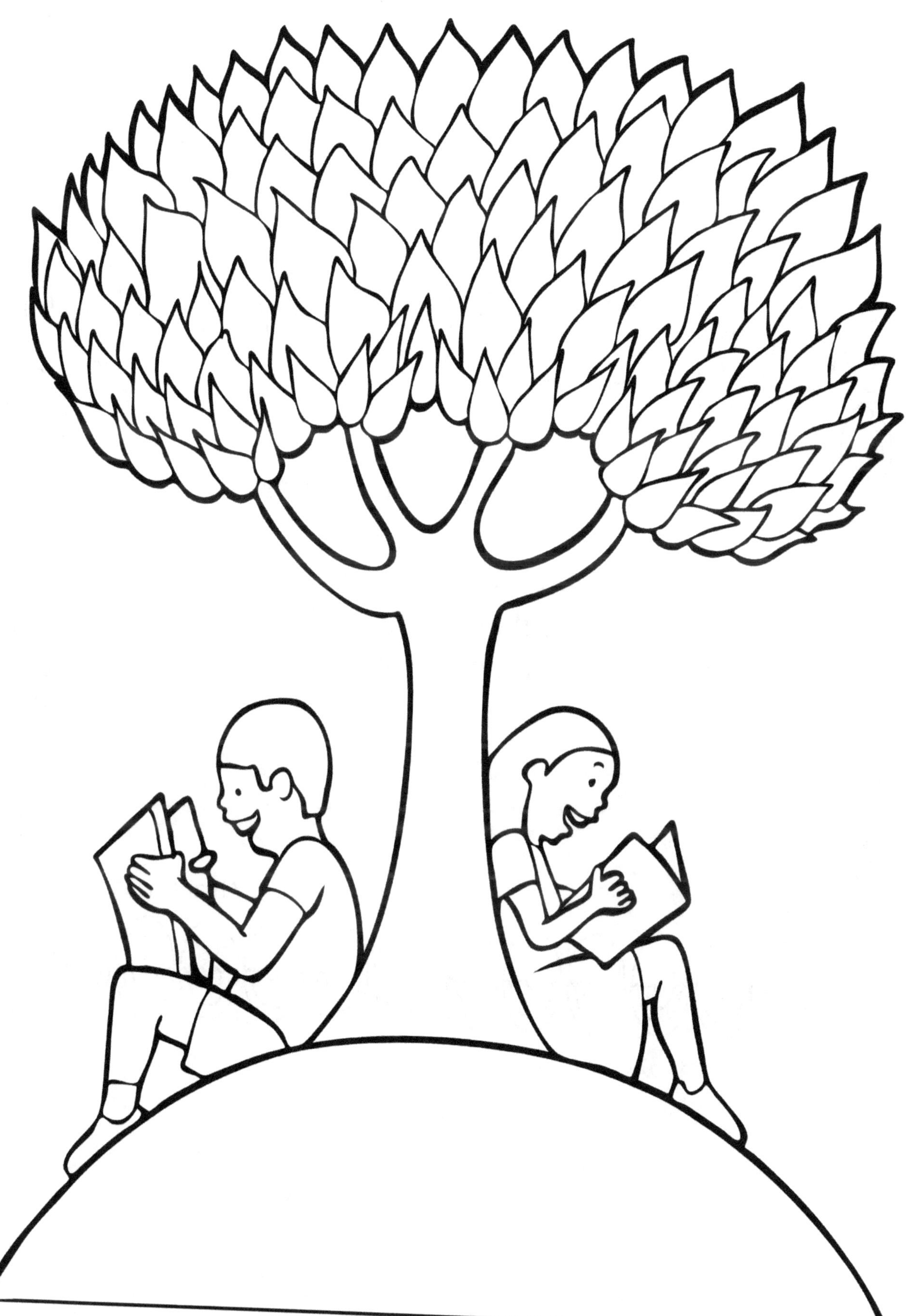

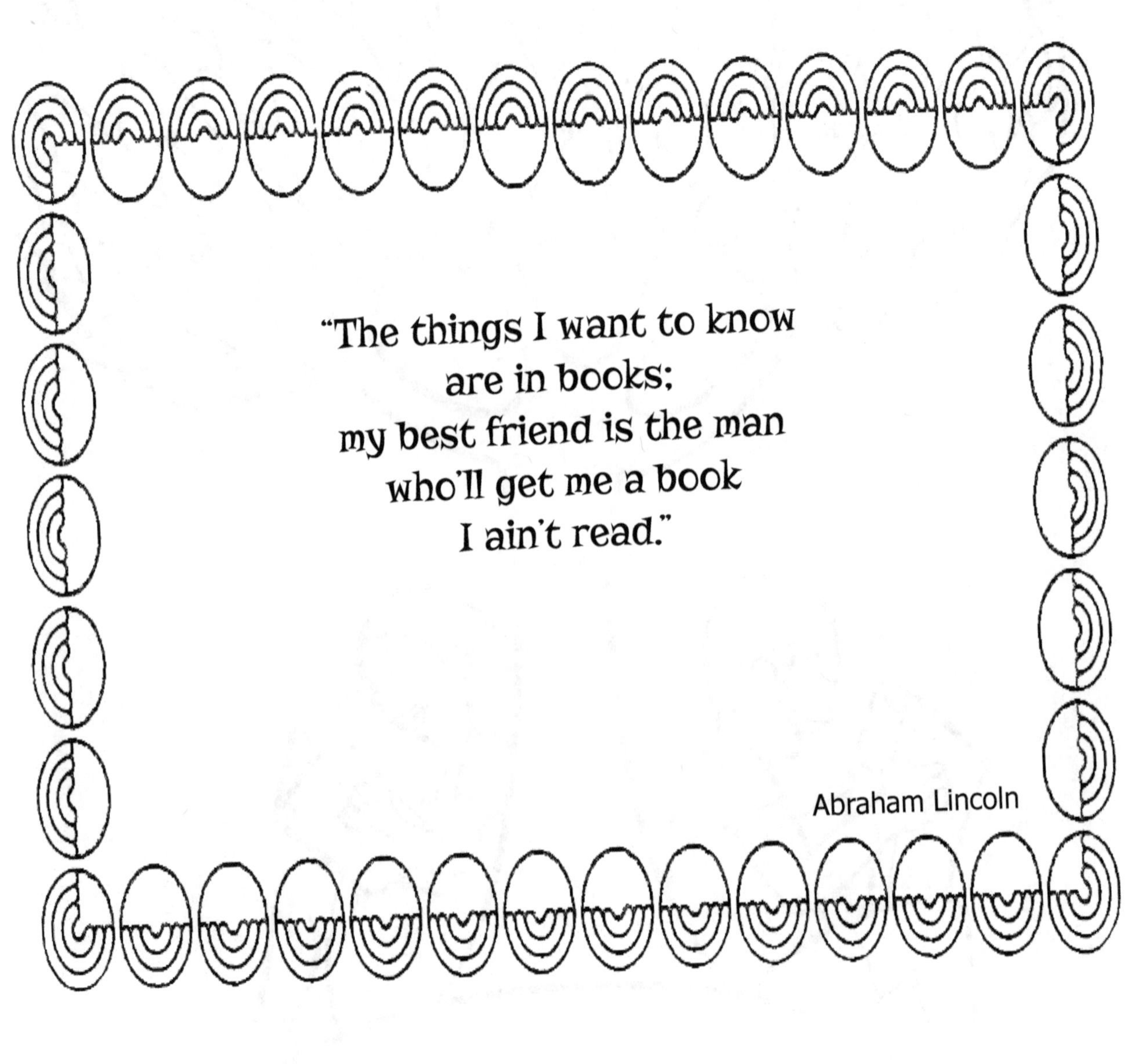
"The things I want to know
are in books;
my best friend is the man
who'll get me a book
I ain't read."
Abraham Lincoln

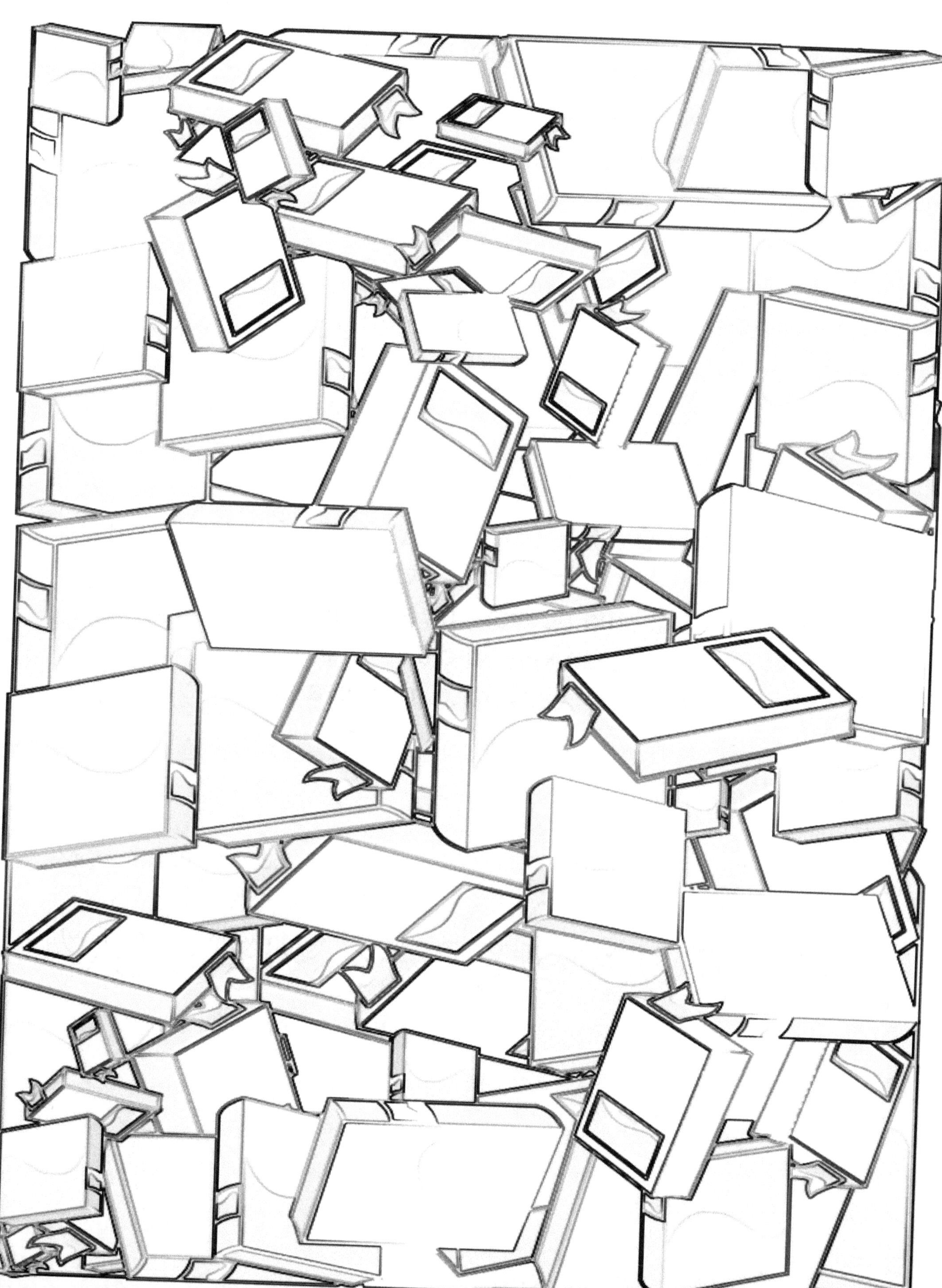

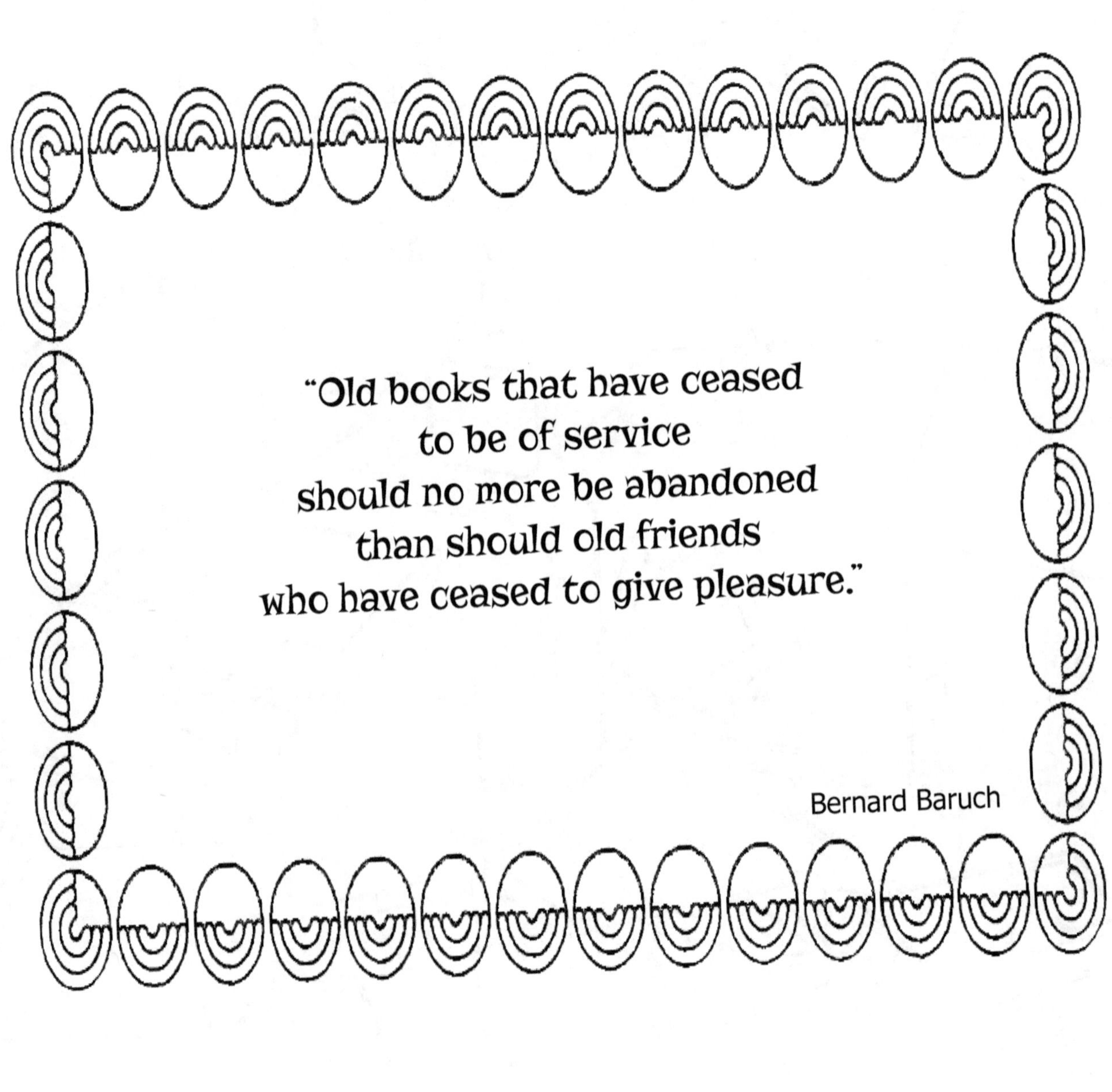
"Old books that have ceased
to be of service
should no more be abandoned
than should old friends
who have ceased to give pleasure."
Bernard Baruch

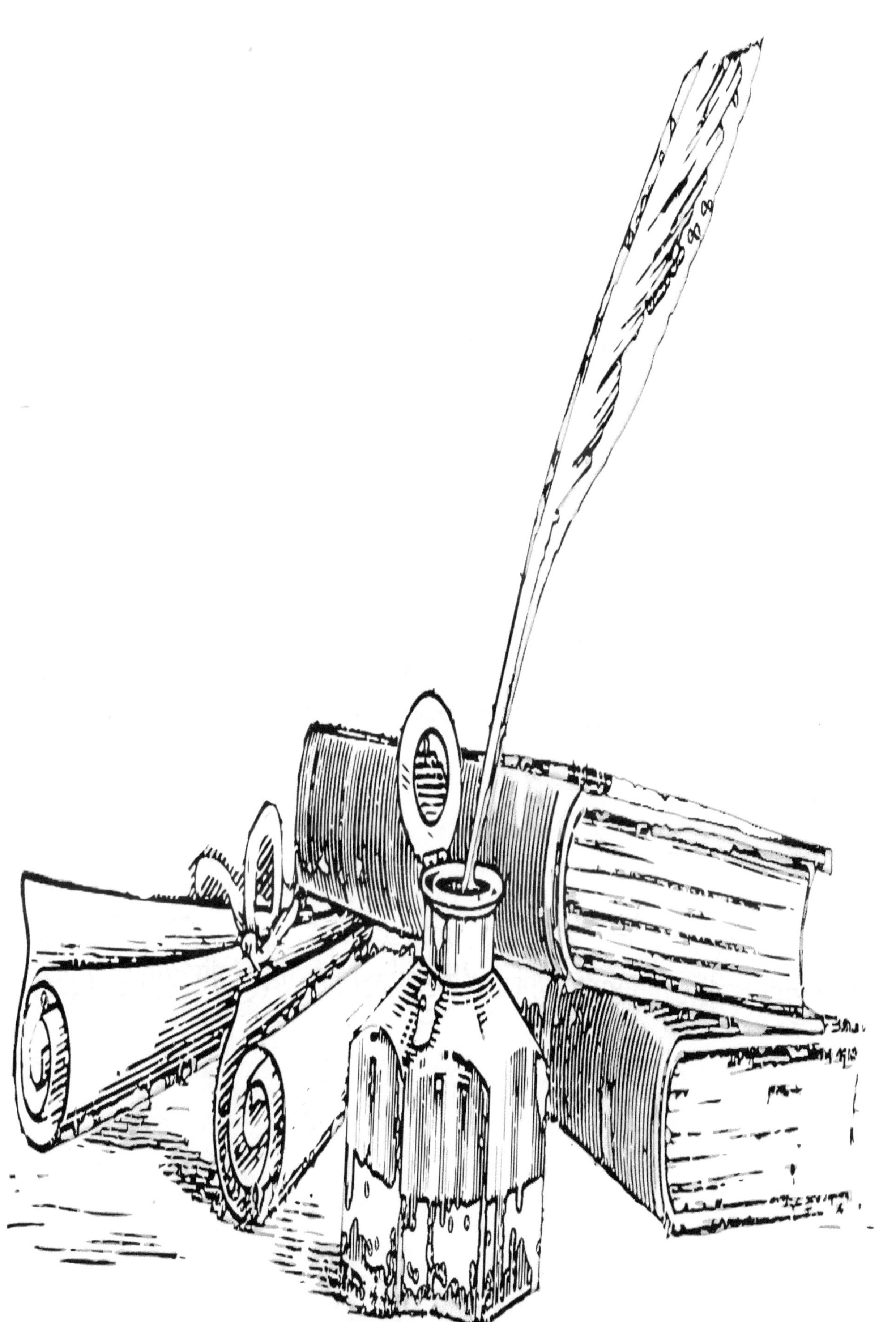

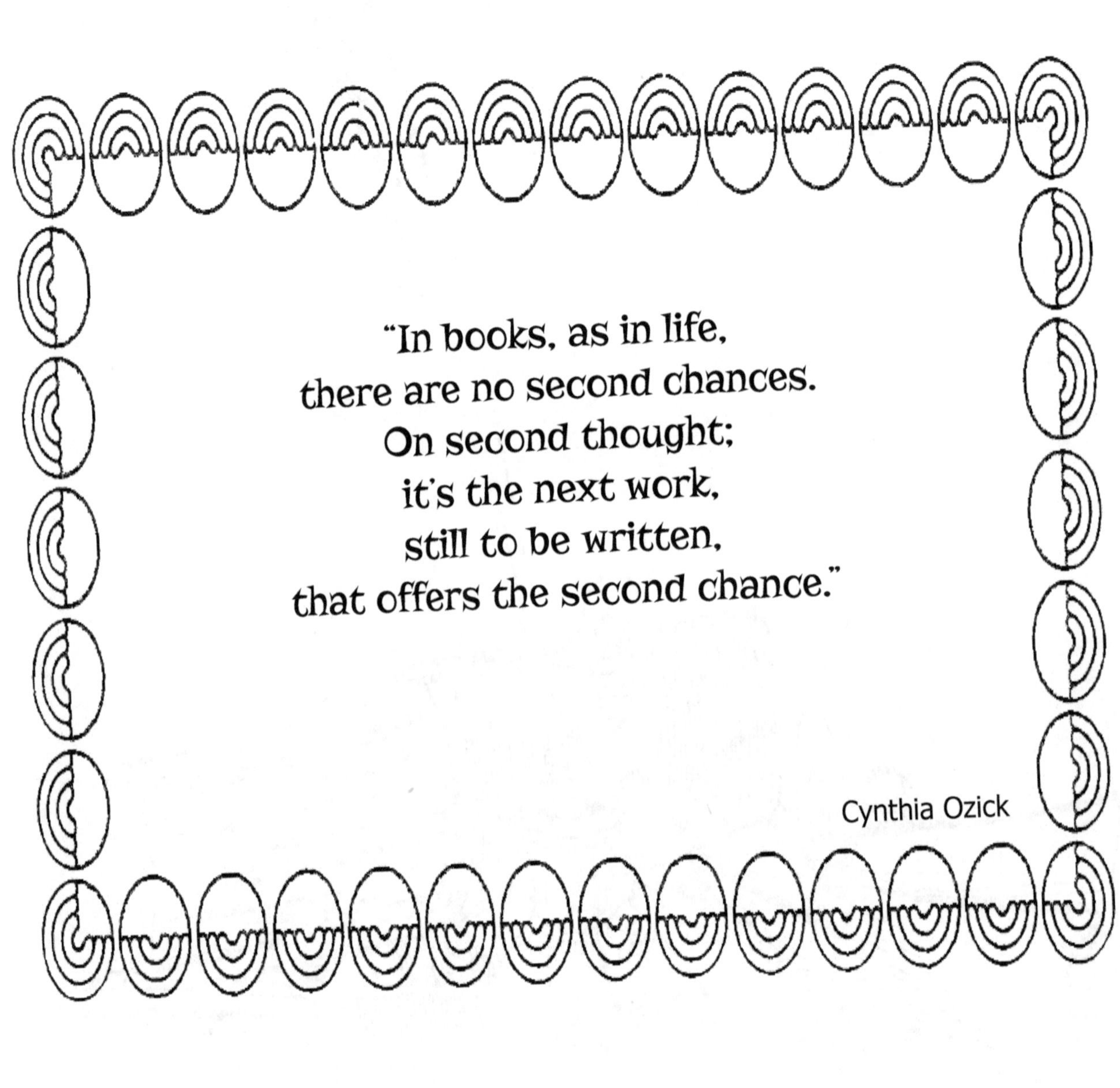

"In books, as in life,
there are no second chances.
On second thought;
it's the next work,
still to be written,
that offers the second chance."

Cynthia Ozick

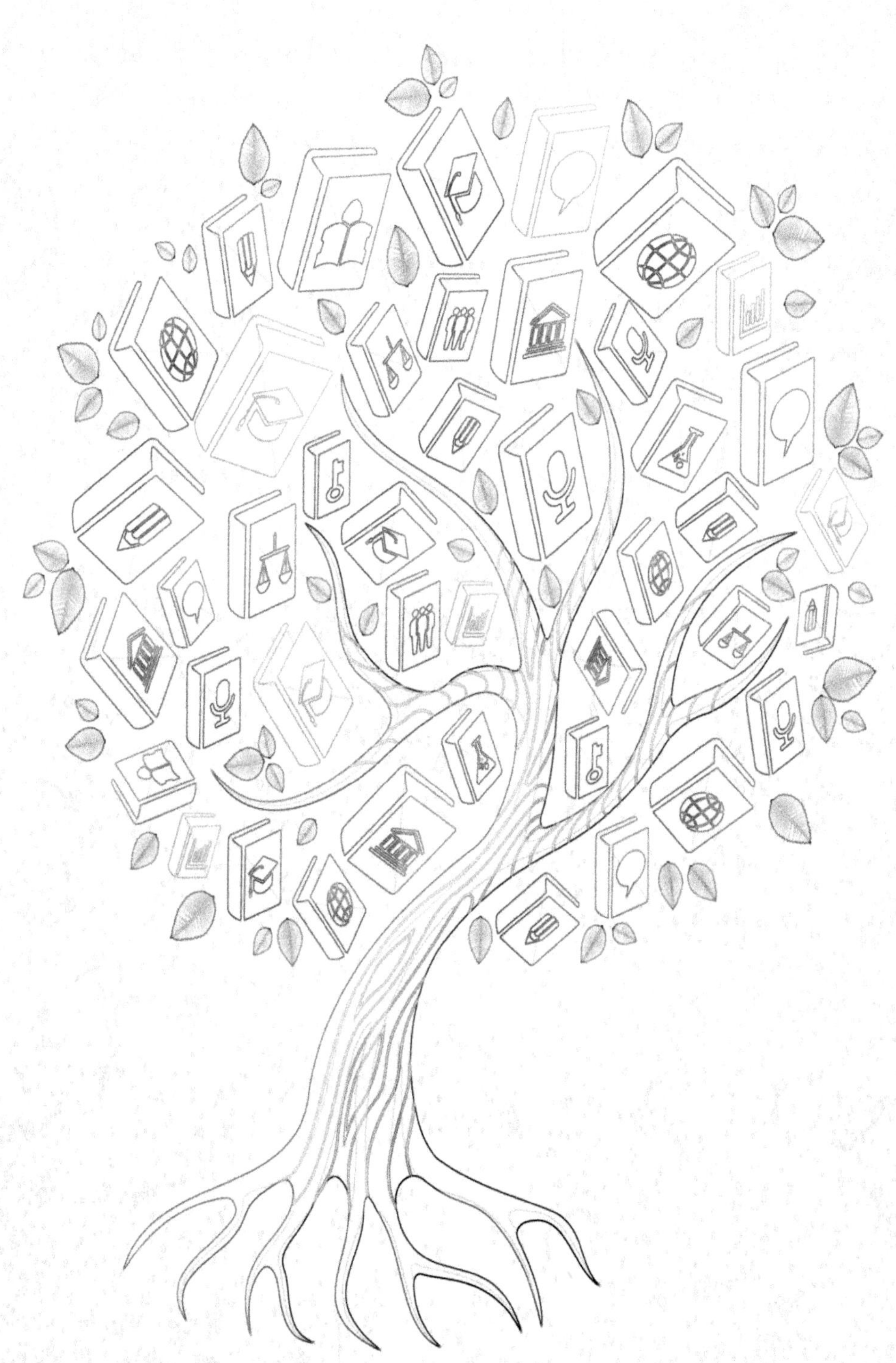

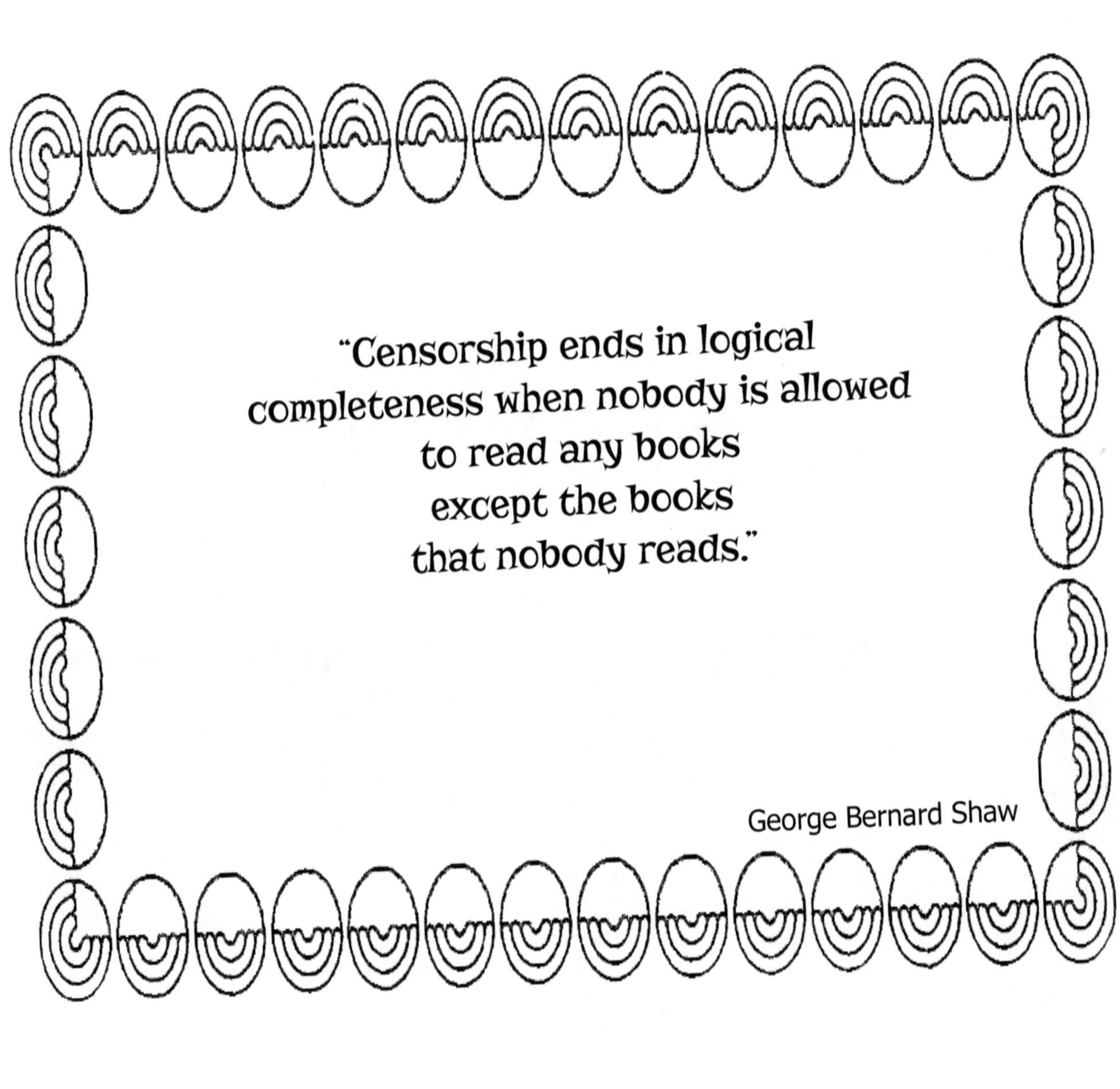

"Censorship ends in logical completeness when nobody is allowed to read any books except the books that nobody reads."

George Bernard Shaw

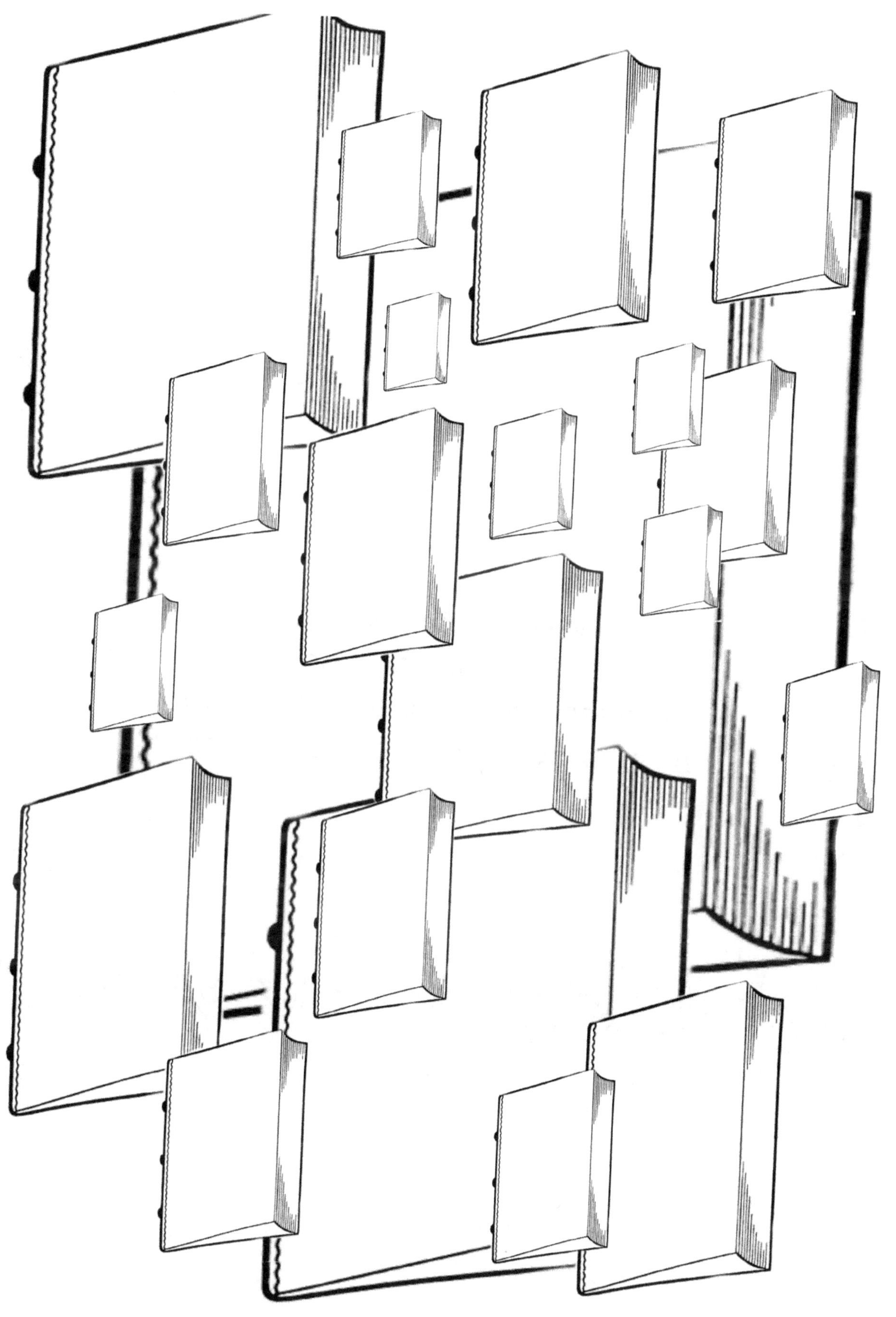

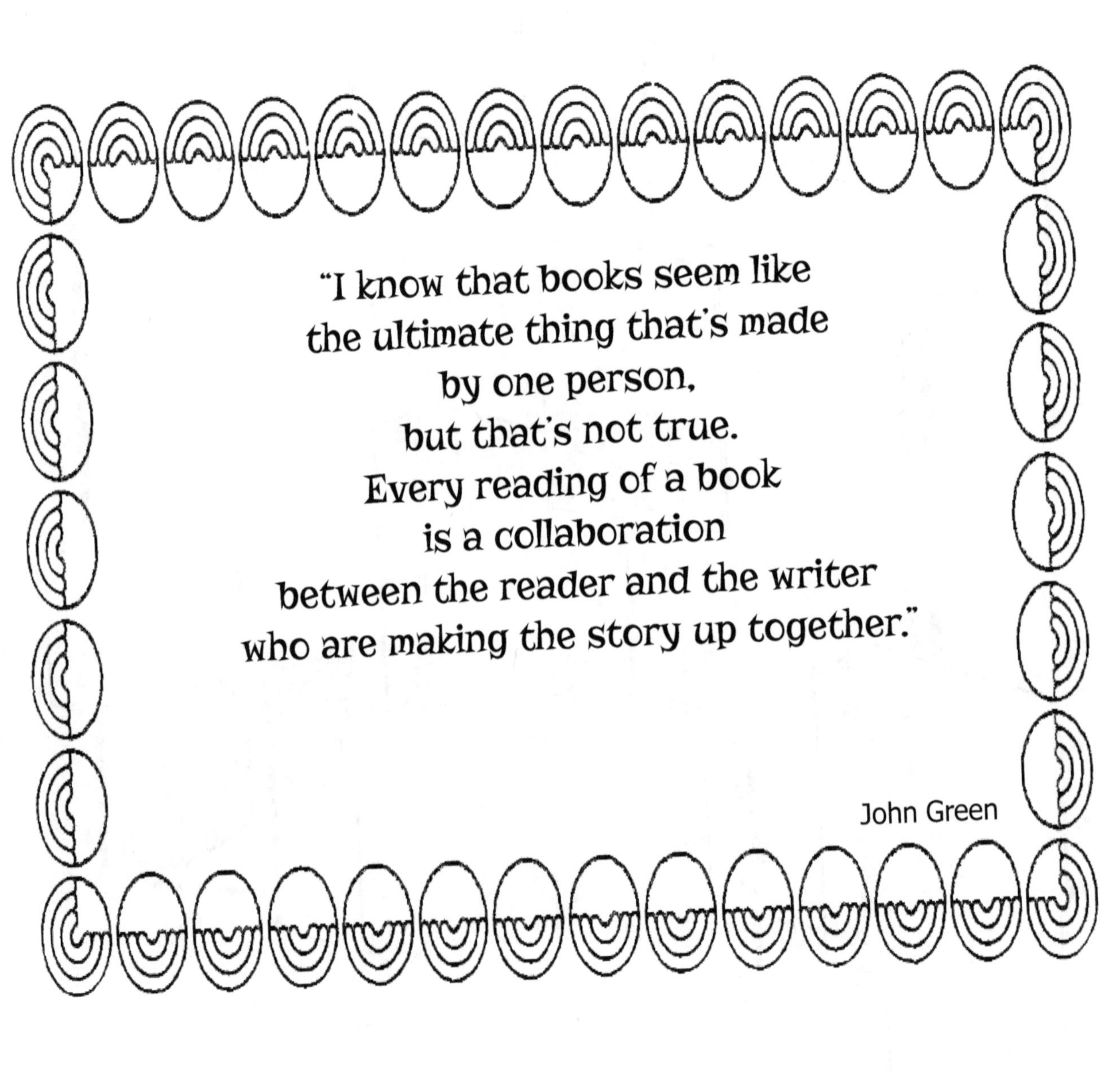

"I know that books seem like
the ultimate thing that's made
by one person,
but that's not true.
Every reading of a book
is a collaboration
between the reader and the writer
who are making the story up together."

John Green

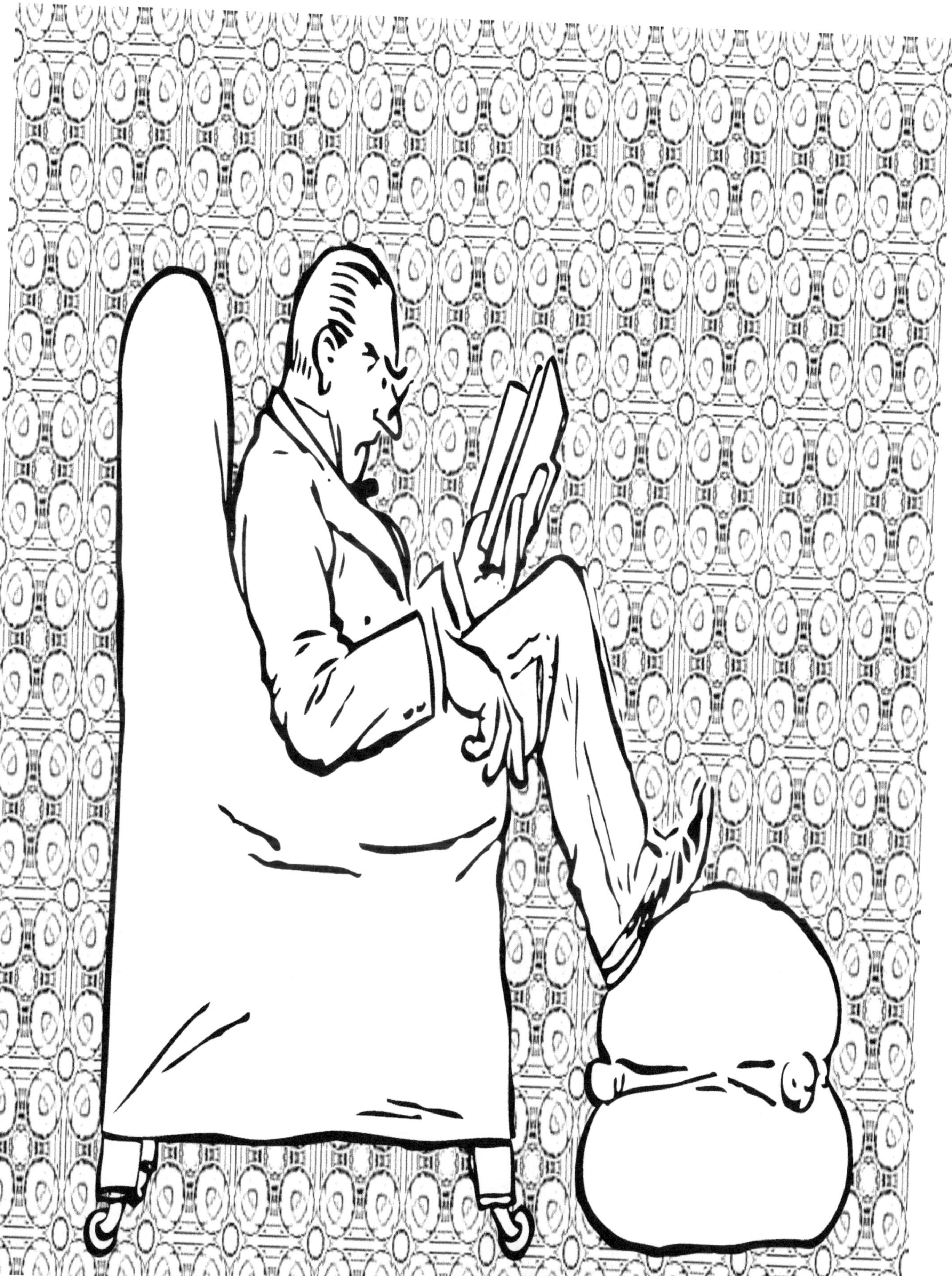

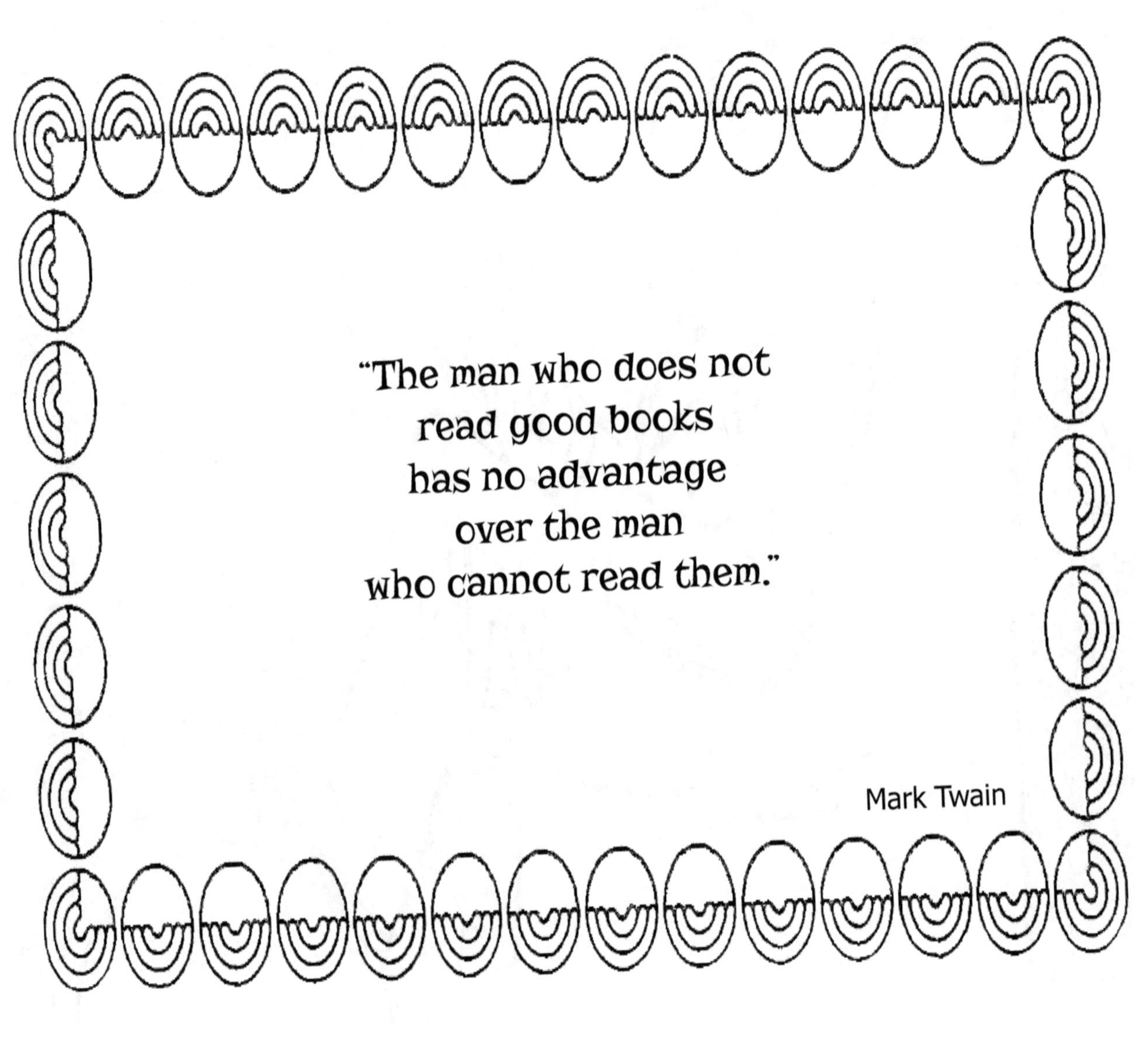

"The man who does not
read good books
has no advantage
over the man
who cannot read them."

Mark Twain

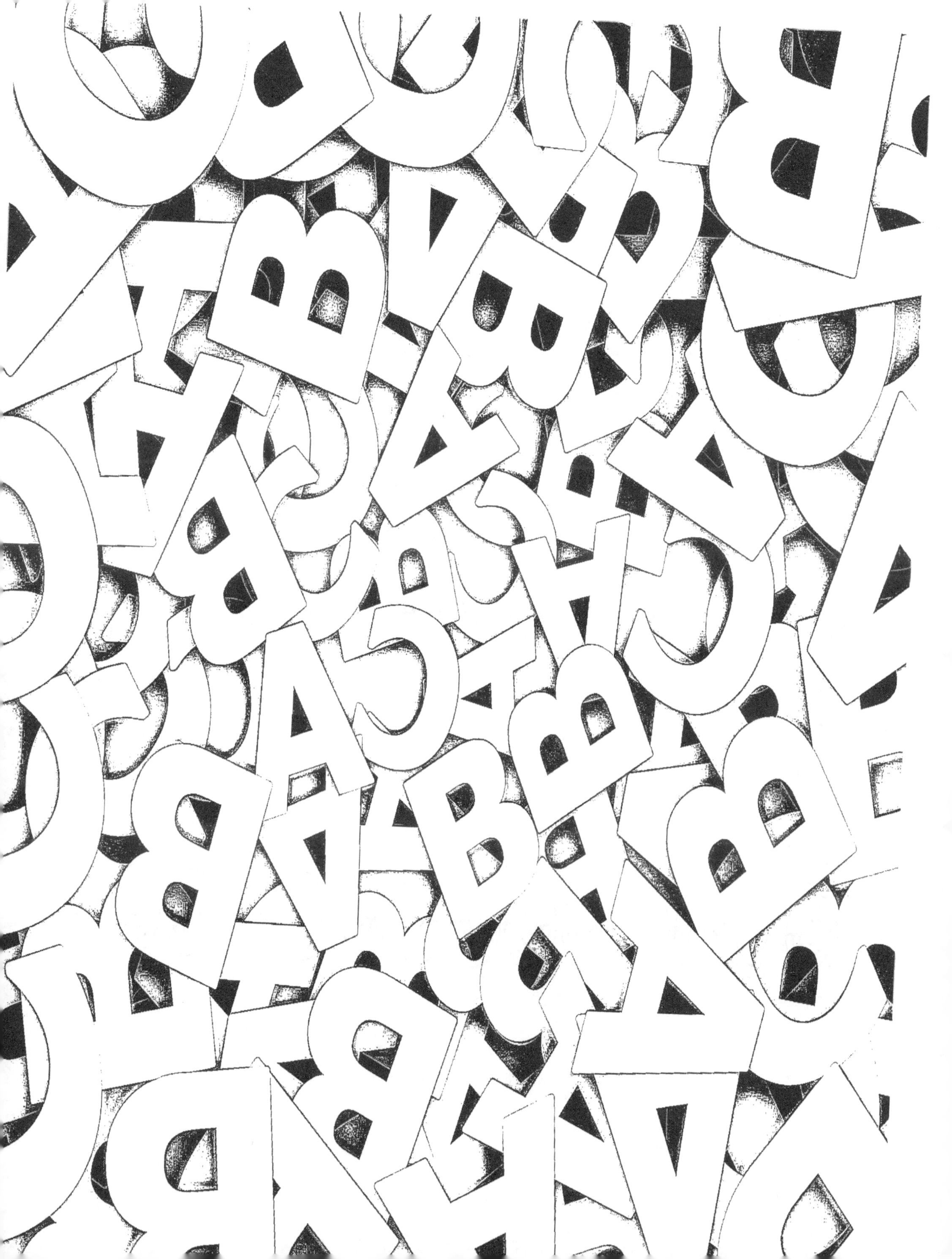

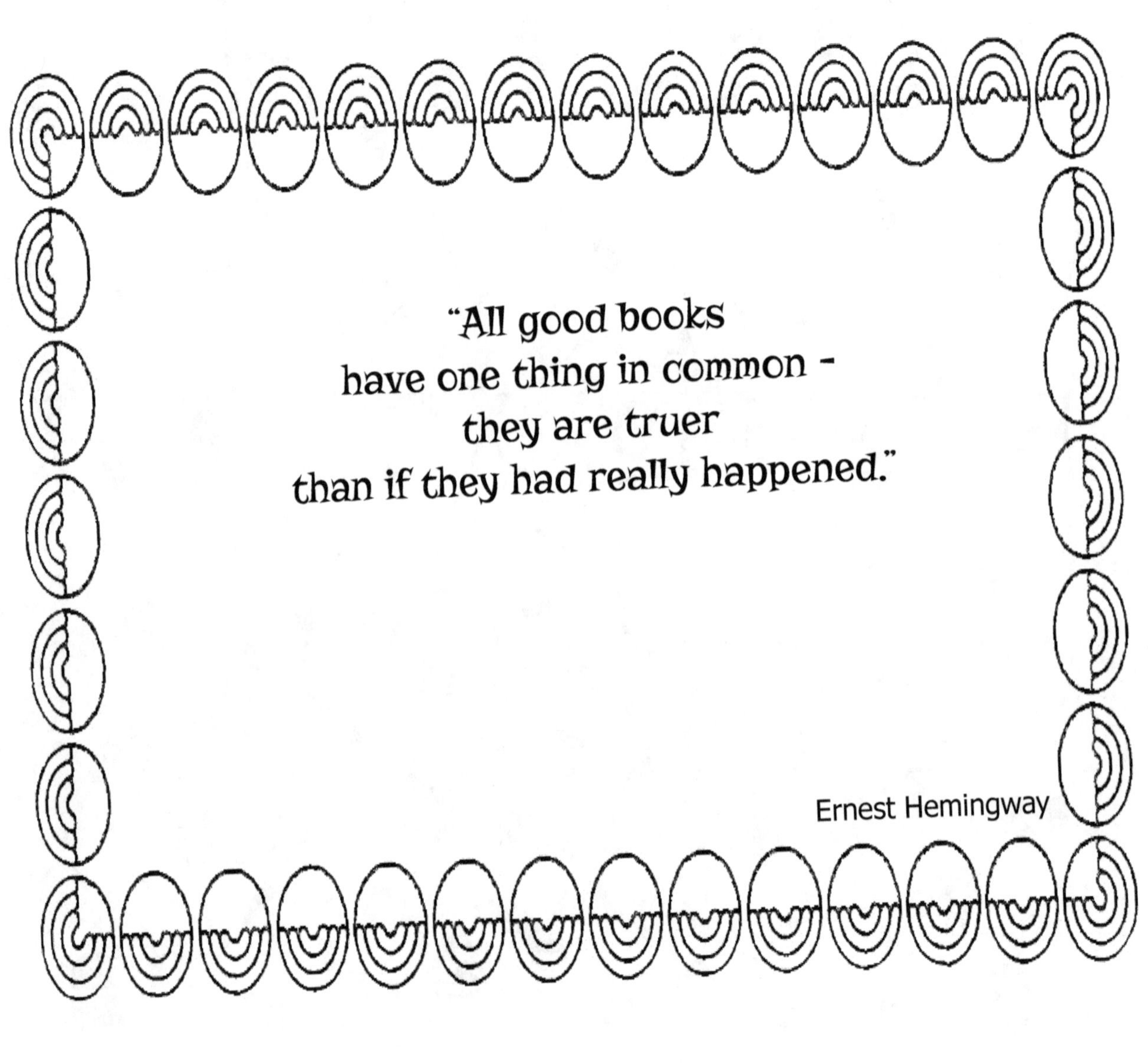
"All good books
have one thing in common -
they are truer
than if they had really happened."
Ernest Hemingway

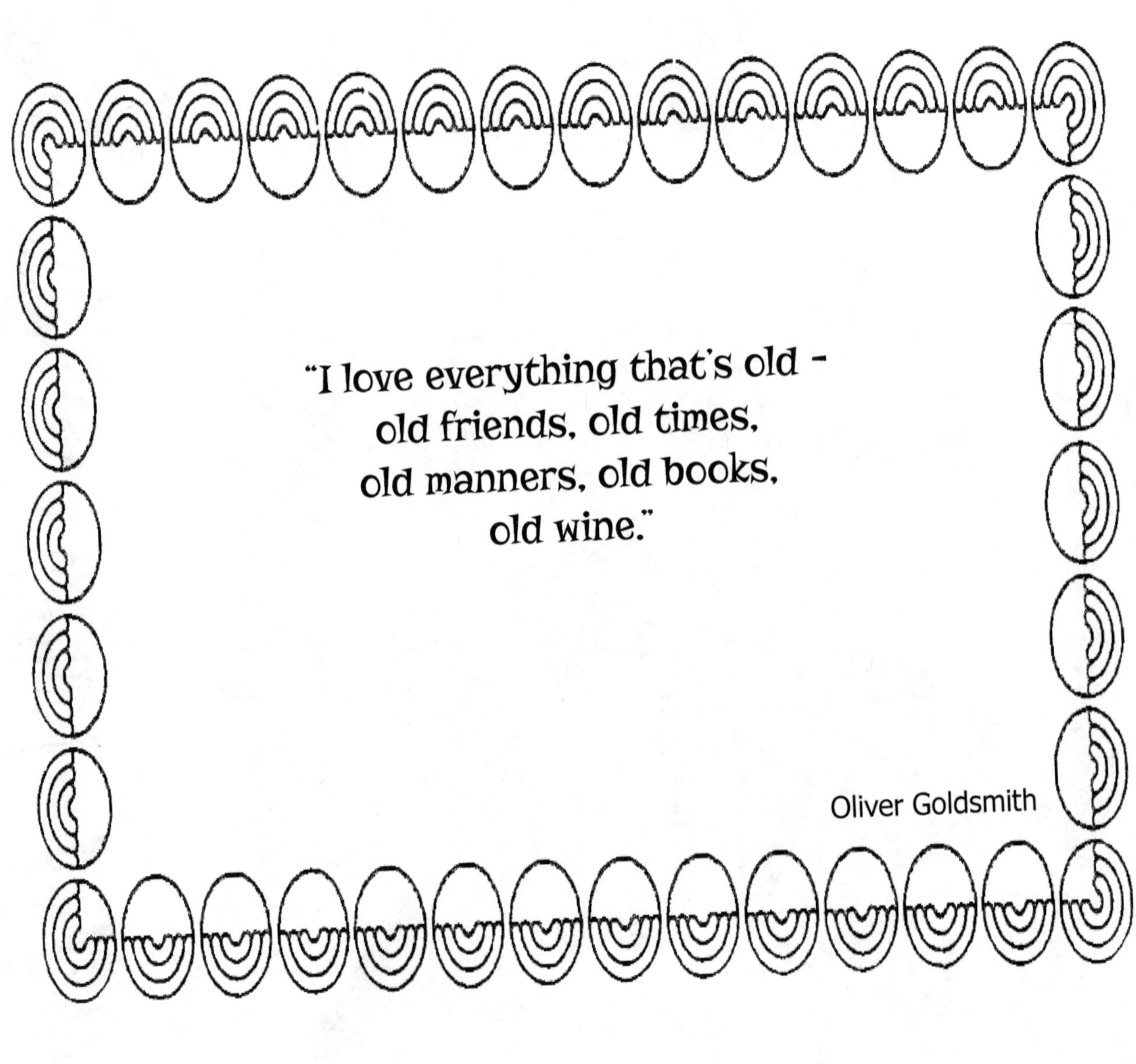
"I love everything that's old -
old friends, old times,
old manners, old books,
old wine."
Oliver Goldsmith

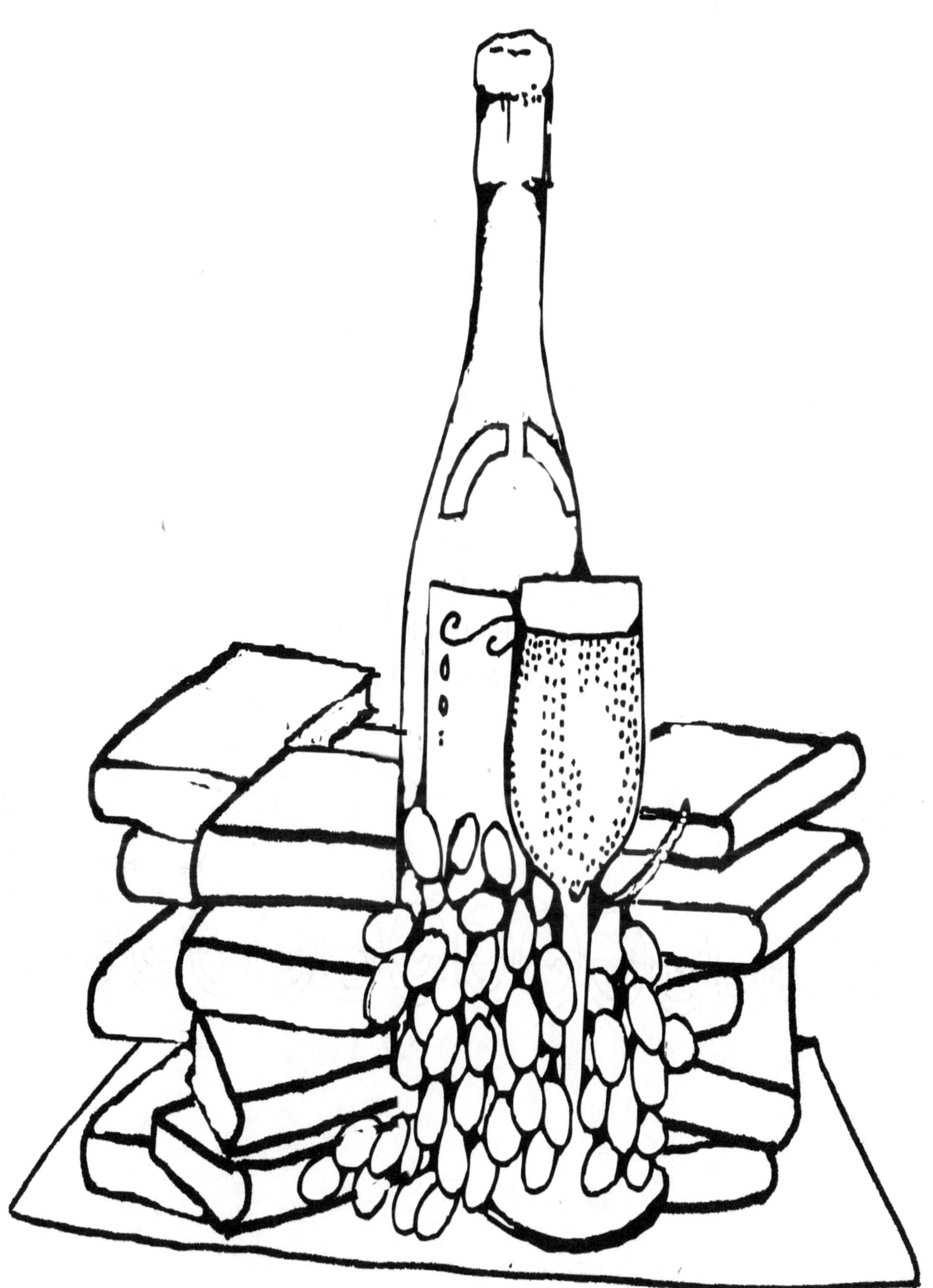

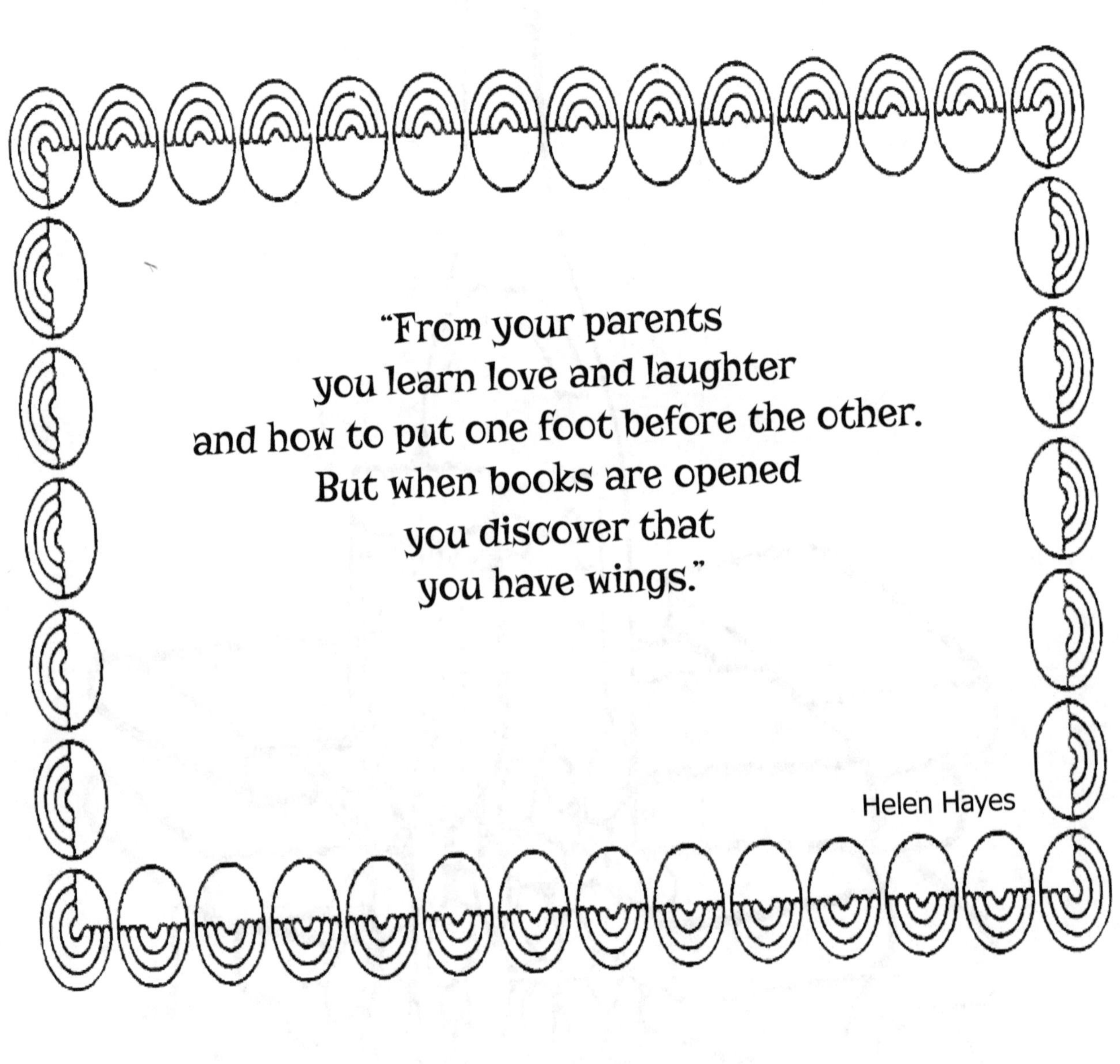

"From your parents
you learn love and laughter
and how to put one foot before the other.
But when books are opened
you discover that
you have wings."

Helen Hayes

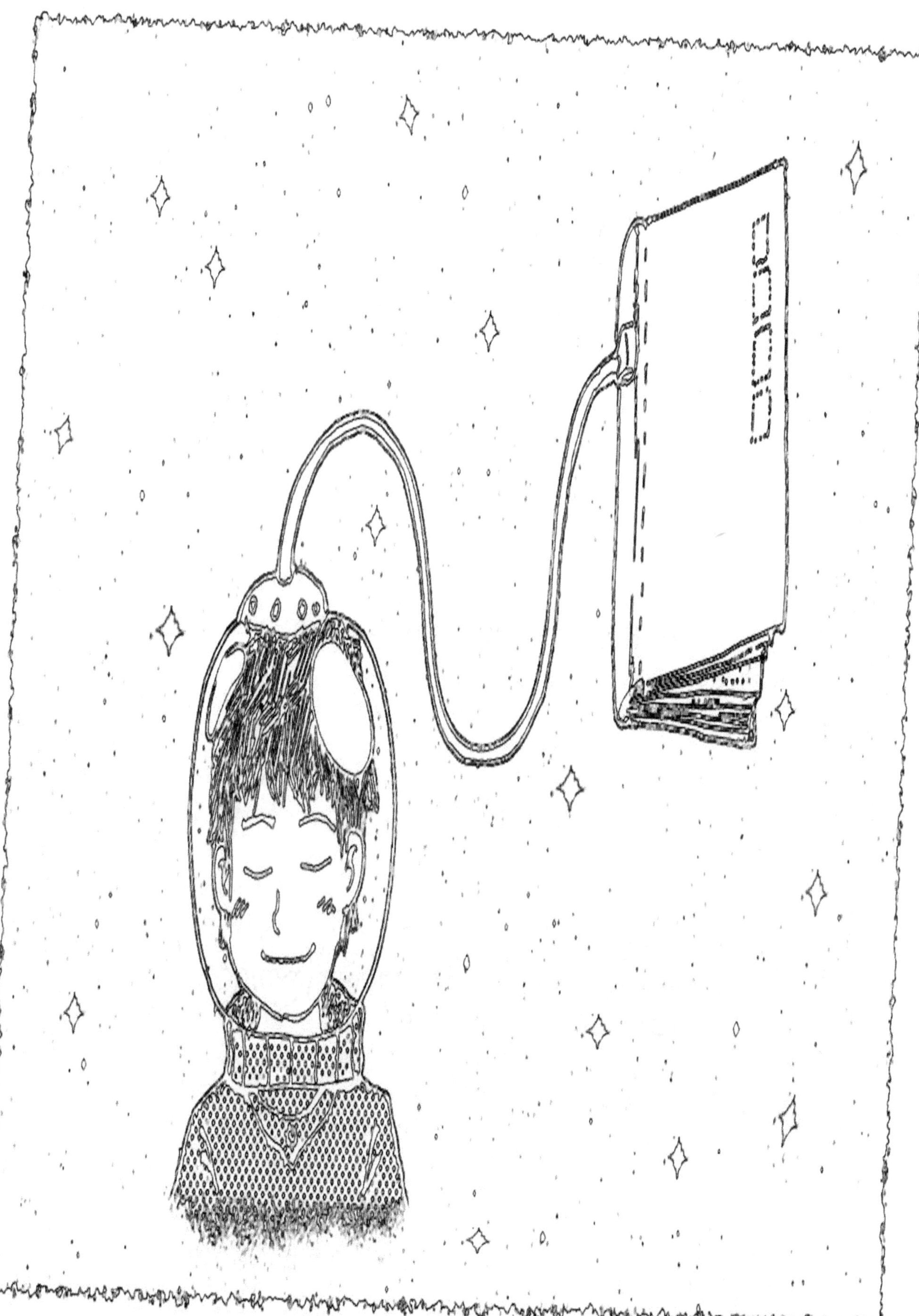

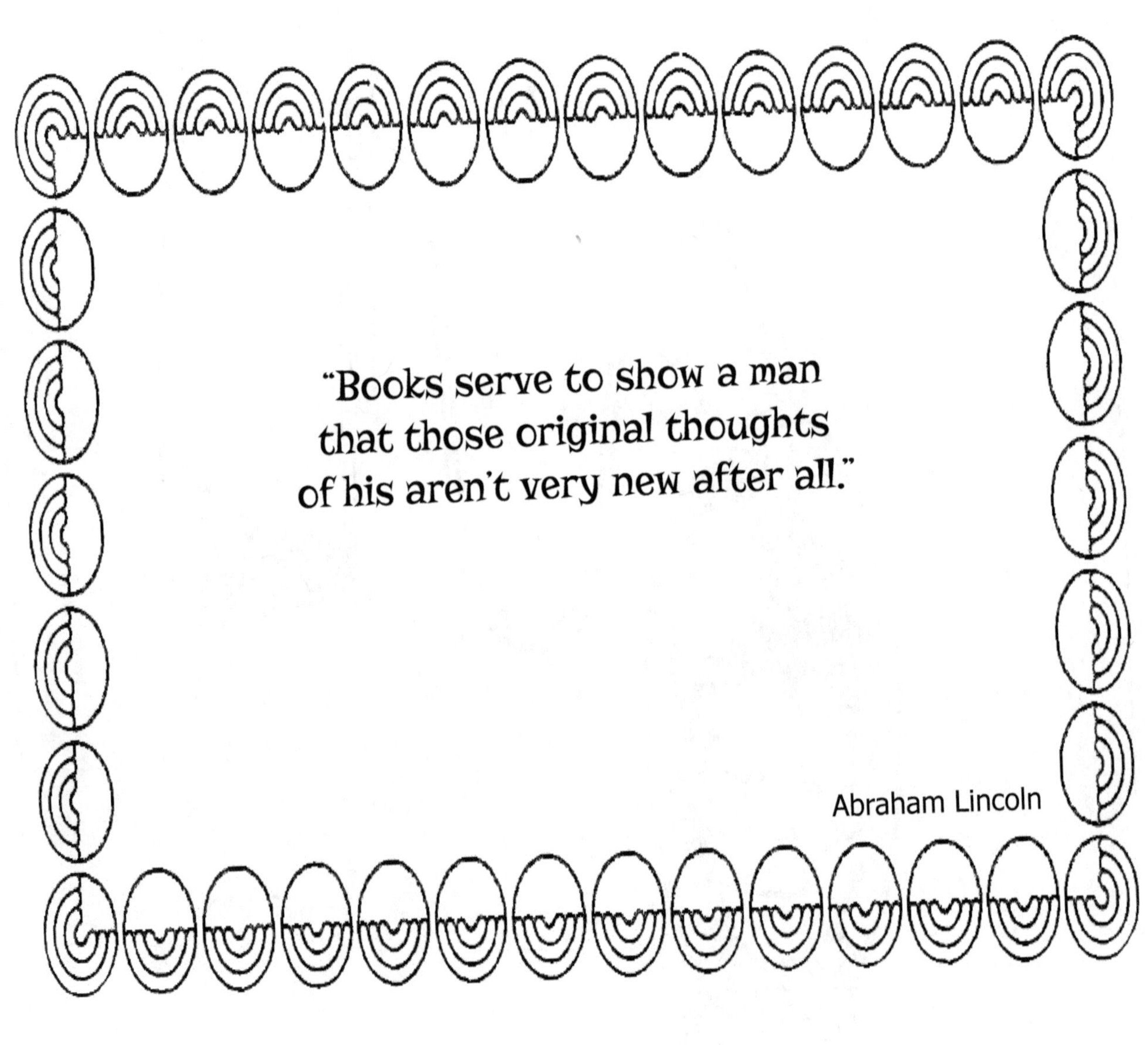
"Books serve to show a man
that those original thoughts
of his aren't very new after all."
Abraham Lincoln

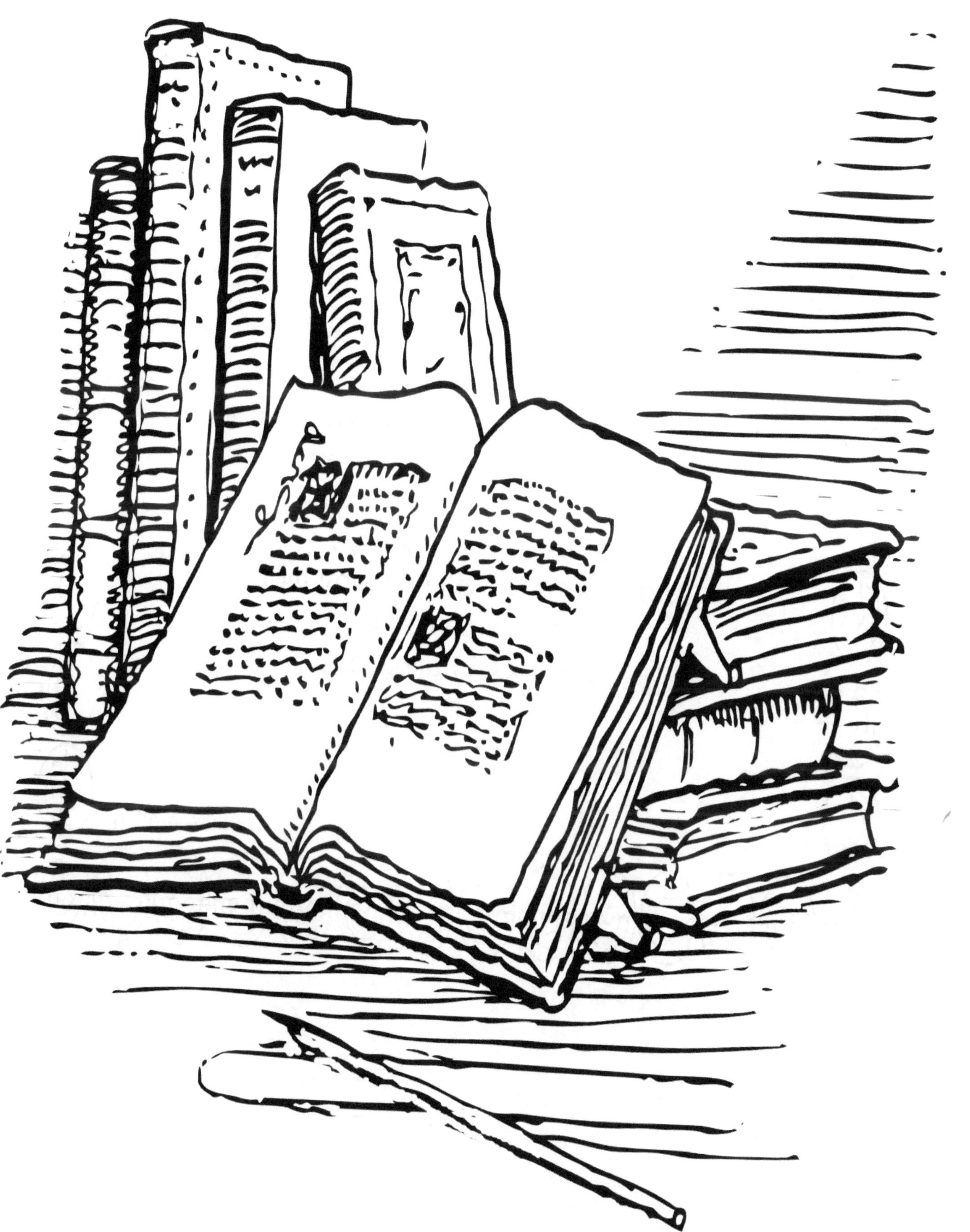

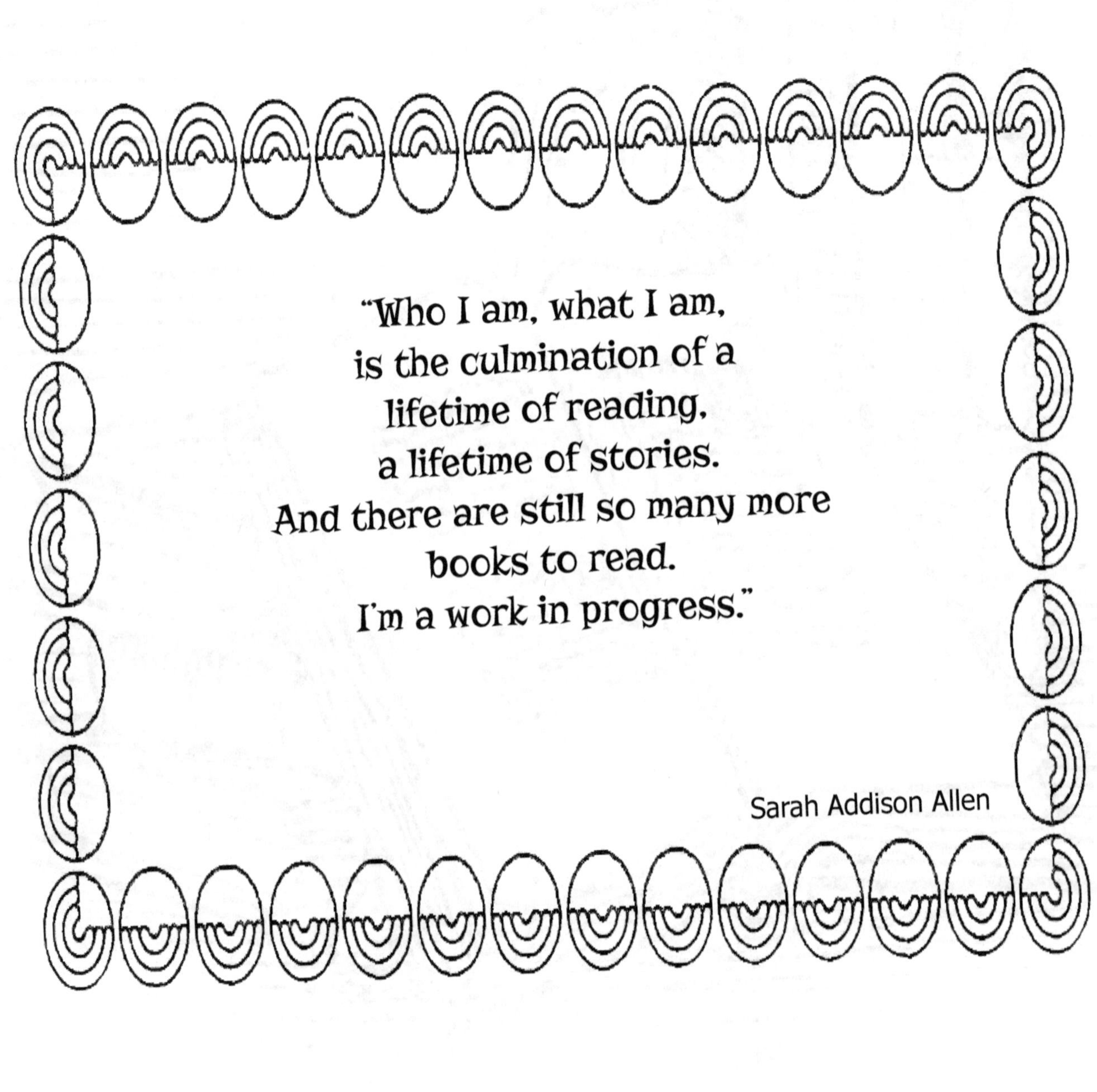
"Who I am, what I am,
is the culmination of a
lifetime of reading,
a lifetime of stories.
And there are still so many more
books to read.
I'm a work in progress."
Sarah Addison Allen

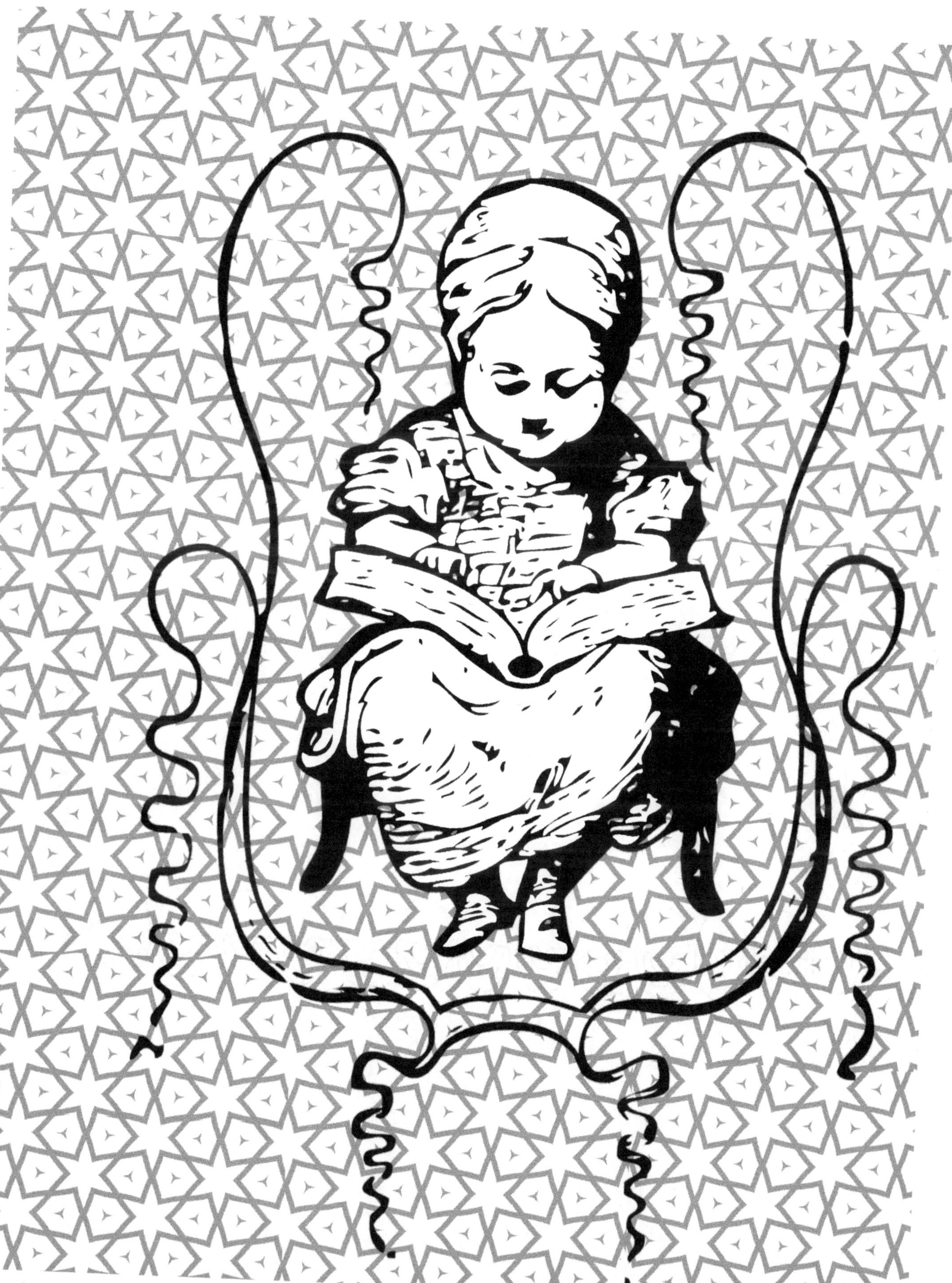

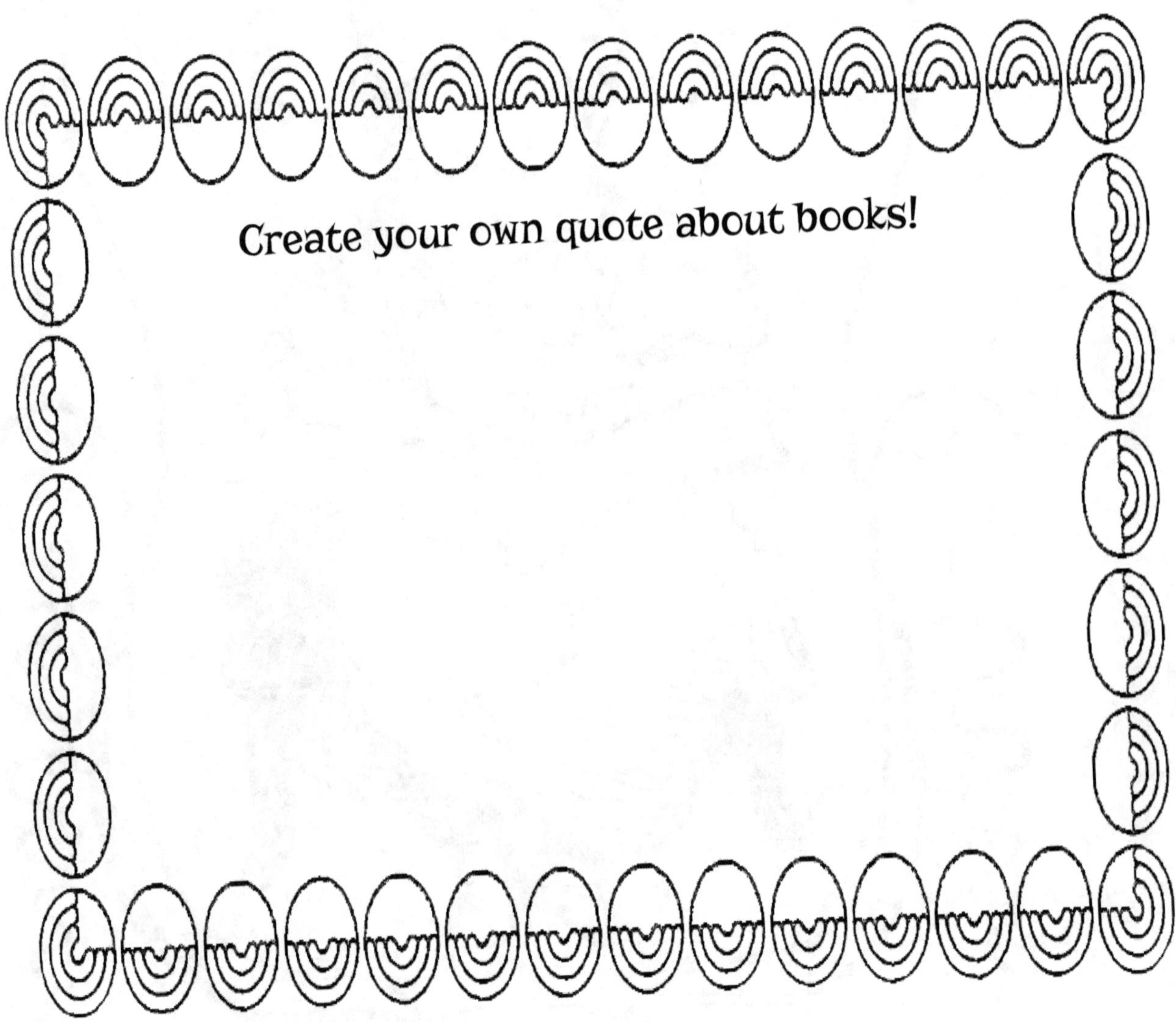
Create your own quote about books!

Dear Coloring Enthusiast,

Thank you for spending time with the Coloring Books Coloring Book. I hope you were amazed with your coloring and had some fun along the way. Creating journals, activity and coloring books is as much of a joy for me as bringing stories to life. Coloring fans like you spark the energy needed to continue creating and telling my tales of romance with a sparkling twist. Again, thank you.

With today's world of vast choices, word of mouth is the best advertising. So please let others know about this journal. Tell your friends, relatives, acquaintances, the dog next door (hey, you never know...). And if you're so inclined, please leave a review, so others can discover The Coloring Books Coloring Book, The Cosmos Journals and the worlds of *lizzie starr.

To keep up with new releases of journals, coloring books and, of course, my fiction, sign up for News From The Starr. Yes, it's a newsletter, but will appear in your email only occasionally. Your email is safe with me, will never be shared, and you can, of course, unsubscribe at any time.

Sign up on my website: www.lizziestarr.com

Continue to always enjoy the love and discovery of Coloring!

*lizzie

The Cosmos Journals

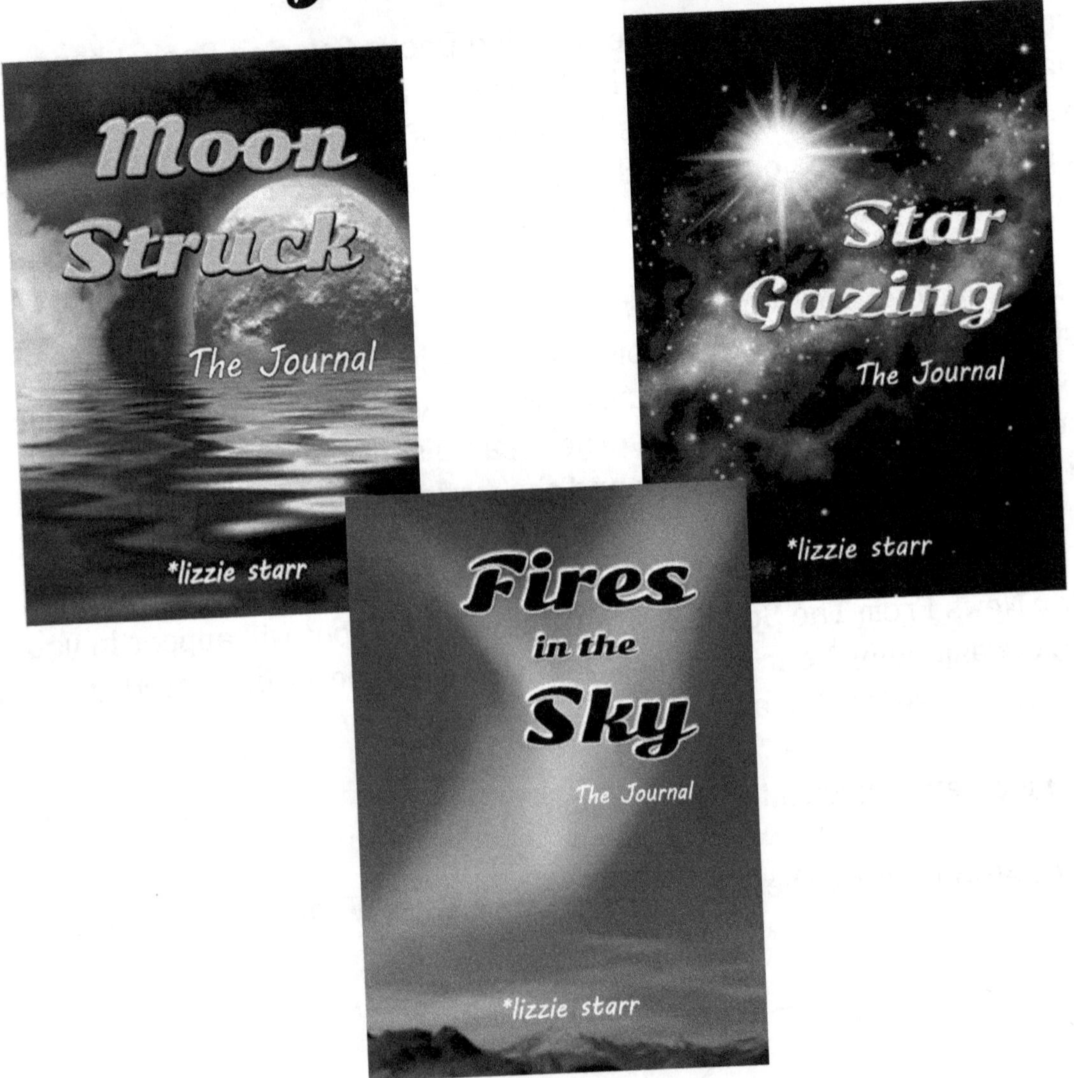

Coming Soon:

Galaxies

Expanding Universes

Meet *lizzie starr

*lizzie always made up games and stories to keep her company. So, a cunning witch lived in Grampa's weather research station and was only held at bay by waving a certain weed. An ancient road grader morphed into a boat carrying wild adventurers to islands filled with fierce lions and dangerous cannibals, which really looked a lot like sheep. Now, filled with fantasy, love, and romance with a sparkling twist, the stories of her imagination swirl their way into the mundane world.

When *lizzie must return to a more routine life, she's *the Lunch Lady* at a private school.

Author and lunch lady~~what a combination!

You can learn more about *lizzie and her novels filled with fanatasy and *romance with a sparkling twist* at www.lizziestarr.com

The Double Keltic Triad
(Fantasy Romance)

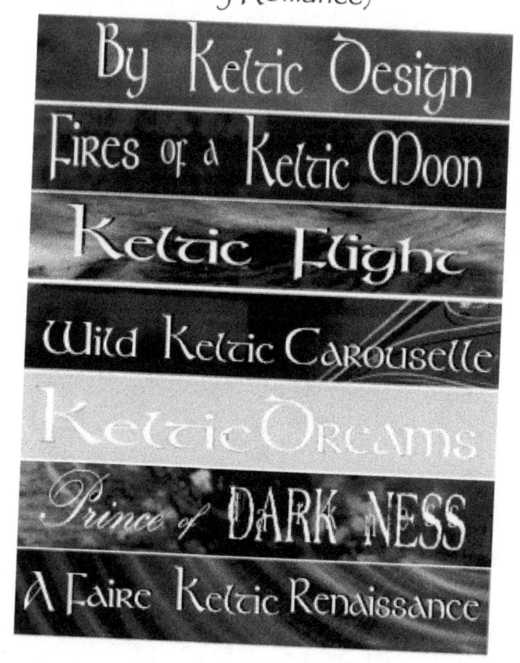

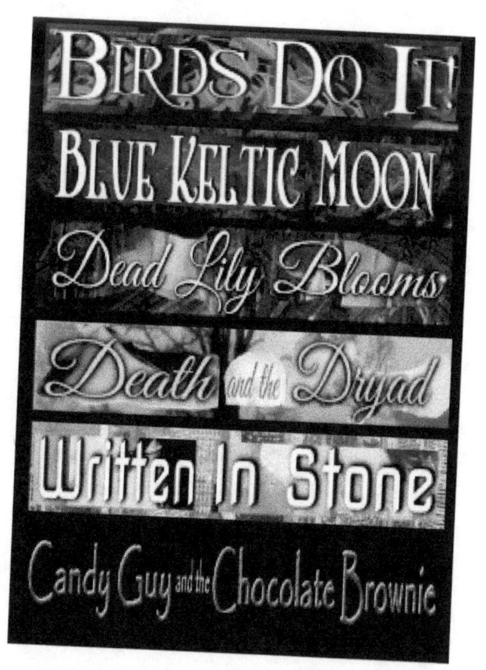

Bonus Coloring Page!

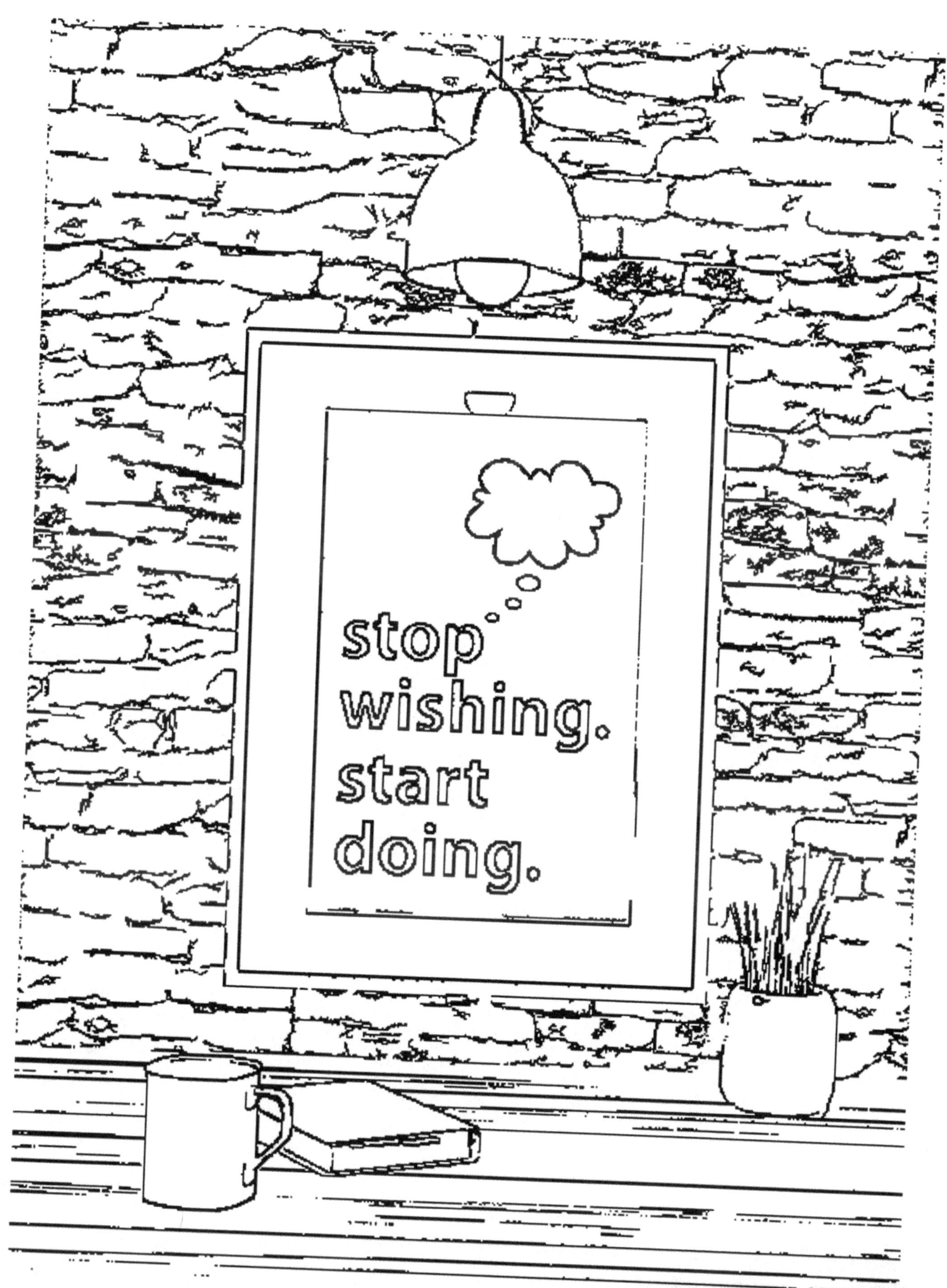
stop
wishing.
start
doing.

www.ingramcontent.com/pod-product-compliance
Lightning Source LLC
LaVergne TN
LVHW081325110826
845149LV00007B/1603